BELONGING

A Memoir

Other Books by Robert W. Fuller

Mathematics of Classical and Quantum Physics
(with Frederick W. Byron, Jr.)

Somebodies and Nobodies: Overcoming the Abuse of Rank

All Rise: Somebodies, Nobodies, and the Politics of Dignity

Dignity for All: How to Create a World Without Rankism
(with Pamela A. Gerloff)

Religion and Science: A Beautiful Friendship?

Genomes, Menomes, Wenomes: Neuroscience and Human Dignity

The Rowan Tree: A Novel

BELONGING

A Memoir

Robert W Fuller

Cover photo credit: Dieter Froese

ISBN: 1493519018
ISBN-13: 978-1493519019

Robert W. Fuller's web site: www.robertworksfuller.com
Dignity Movement: www.breakingranks.net
Huffington Post: www.huffingtonpost.com/robert-fuller

§§§

For readers who want to explore dignity as a foundation for interpersonal and international relations, Robert W. Fuller's novel *The Rowan Tree* is now available as an ebook, a paperback, and an audiobook at: **www.rowantreenovel.com**

To Arlene

It is long ere we discover how rich we are. Our history, we are sure, is quite tame. We have nothing to write, nothing to infer. But our wiser years still run back to the despised recollections of childhood, and always we are fishing up some wonderful article out of that pond; until by-and-by we begin to suspect that the biography of the one foolish person we know is in reality, nothing less than the miniature paraphrase of the hundred volumes of the Universal History.

– Ralph Waldo Emerson, from *Intellect*

Table of Contents

Prologue | Quests and Questions

Nothing shapes our quests more than our questions. My questions are ones of being, becoming, and belonging. This memoir tells of my search for answers.

Nothing shapes our future more than the stories we tell of our past. These stories have shaped me.

1 | Beginnings
(1936–1945)

Arlene

In the fall of 1943, on the first day of second grade, our teacher had announced two inviolable rules: Each pupil must carry a fresh handkerchief and have clean fingernails. Every morning began with an inspection. One day Arlene failed. Her fingernails were dirty, and Miss Belcher told her to go out into the hall and stay there until her fingernails were clean. I wondered how Arlene could clean her nails in the hall. I pictured her holding her fingers in the water trickling from the drinking fountain and doubted it would work—cold water, no soap.

Later, as the class filed out for recess, we snuck glances at Arlene. Standing alone, slumped against the wall, hiding her face, she shrank from our snickers. She was the smallest kid in our class, and I can still picture her running to catch the school bus when it stopped near the farm where her father labored. She was tiny and thin and wore the same faded plaid dress every day. Most kids bounded onto the bus, greeting their friends, but Arlene struggled up the steps, averting her eyes and sitting by herself.

When I got home I told my mother what had happened to Arlene, and every morning for the rest of that year she checked to see if my nails were clean and made sure I had a fresh handkerchief. I was never sent to the hall. To this day, I heed Miss Belcher's rules.

The Spinach Standoff

Every family has its legends. One of my family's is *The Spinach Standoff.*

When I was about four I refused to eat the canned spinach my mother set before me. If you've ever seen a Popeye cartoon, you'll remember canned spinach. Whenever Popeye faces a crisis that calls for a muscular solution, he opens a can of spinach and pours it directly down his throat. Canned spinach flows like pond scum.

My refusal to try even a spoonful ran up against the moral my mother had drawn from the Great Depression—that we must lick our platters clean. To break the impasse, she issued a threat: Until you eat the spinach, you get nothing else. When I refused even to try it, I was sent to my room. Every few hours my mother would come to my bedroom door, open it a few inches, and poke a spoonful of the dark slime through the crack.

There's some disagreement about how long this stalemate lasted, but all parties agree that it was at least forty-eight hours. By then the twin pressures of my hunger and my mother's guilt produced a deal: I would part my lips and permit the spoon to enter the hollow of my mouth, but she would withdraw it without my having to swallow its contents. With this deferential gesture, I won release from exile and regained my seat at the dinner table. Canned spinach was never served again. My mother had put me to the test, but in the end she allowed me to save face. Not lost on me was that my gesture of acquiescence enabled her to save hers.

The spinach standoff was not about spinach, or about wasting food. It was about who was boss. It was a struggle over the balance of power in the parent-child relationship. On my side, the issue was personal autonomy, and my weapons were intransigence and guilt-tripping. For my mother, the issue was parental authority, and her weapons were to deprive me of food and recognition, and threaten my sense of belonging. The way the impasse was resolved—by allowing both parties to save face—held a lesson that would serve me in many other contexts.

The lick-your-platter-clean school of culinary discipline was widespread during the Great Depression. Usually it took the form of no dessert until your plate is empty. The explanation "because I say so" was regarded as unimpeachable. Military-style obedience—to a parent, teacher, doctor, or employer—was the norm. Rank ruled, right or wrong, no questions permitted. The bumper sticker "Question Authority" would not appear for decades.

In those days, no public agency would have intervened in a power struggle between parent and child—even one threatening the health of the child, which the spinach standoff did not do. Domestic conflicts of all sorts fell under the umbrella of "nobody's business."

But imagine a deadlock that goes on for a week or more. There comes a point when a parent's authority must be overridden. The difference between proper and improper uses of rank is the difference between the dignity of belonging and the indignity of banishment. Carried to extremes, that can mean the difference between life and death.

My brothers and I were spanked. Physical domination has always been used to establish rank, and bullying has long figured in child rearing. I uncritically adopted this form of discipline with my first child, became ambivalent with the second, and dropped it entirely with the third and fourth. I'm chagrined that, as a young parent, I mindlessly accepted such brutal social norms.

Our Town

Chatham sat on the border between rural and suburban New Jersey, about twenty miles west of New York City and a few miles from Bell Telephone Laboratories, where my father worked. Many of my classmates' fathers commuted to white collar jobs in New York City. Most of our mothers saw themselves as housewives and homemakers, not as wage-earners.

My classmates were a mix of religions—Protestants, Catholics, and Jews—but religion didn't matter to us. Race wasn't much of an issue either, because all of us were white. I learned later that realtors conspired to keep non-whites out of Chatham.

Up until second grade we all seemed pretty much alike to each other—just a bunch of kids, blind to things like religion, race, class, and our varying aptitudes. None of us had yet separated from the pack.

But about this time a powerful distinction began to creep into our judgments of one another—the distinction between "smart" kids and "dumb" kids. I couldn't tell whether Arlene was smart or dumb because she hardly ever spoke, and then only in a whisper. But I could tell that Miss Belcher thought she, as well as some of my friends, were dumb. I was unsure about dumb and smart, because although this difference seemed real enough in class, I saw no evidence for it on the playground or after school. I kept my doubts to myself because *everyone* knew who the dumb kids were.

Band of Brothers and Sisters

My classmates and I formed a tight little band, moving each year from one room to the next in the nine-room school exactly as our predecessors had done for decades. By the time we reached the upper grades we knew each other like brothers and sisters.[1]

The teachers taught the same class every year so you knew in advance that in first grade you'd have Mrs. Vail; in second grade, Miss Belcher; in third grade, Mrs. Bahoosian; in fourth grade, Miss Stetler (whose transformation into Mrs. Walker during the year was an eye-opener); and so on.

As we advanced from kindergarten to eighth grade (Mr. Van Cise), I watched as more of my classmates suffered shame and failure, and gradually reconciled themselves to their place in the academic hierarchy. As one of the survivors, I sometimes tried to help classmates with math and science. I noticed then that even when they understood something perfectly well in our private sessions this did not always translate into performance on a test.

By third grade, our relative positions had jelled. I sensed an arbitrariness in the ranking and remember encouraging several of my friends to resist their relegation. I could not then make out the obstacles that stood in their way, and tended to dismiss their explanations for their difficulties as excuses. But gradually I sensed that some invisible, implacable force was grinding them down.

By fourth grade, there was no denying that we'd been sorted into two piles—dumb kids and smart kids—the first group larger than the second. Since there were no black kids, correlations between color and aptitude never gained a foothold. There were, however, quite visible *class* differences, and I noticed that none of the kids from high-status families ended up in the dumb group. Their failures were laughed off and then excused as part of growing up. Their ultimate success was assured. Some of the poor kids had shown promise early on, but by the time we were in high school it was clear that most of us would follow in our parents' footsteps.

My classmates' successes and failures intrigued me. What was it like for Arlene in the hall? What kept Sandra from seeing that 3 x 4 = 4 x 3? How could Gordon draw cars that looked like magazine illustrations? How did Linda play the piano without a score? Why did Tom always read while he ate? What did it mean that a condom dropped out the cuff of Arthur's pants? And how was it that Jerry, the class dunce, was the only one of us to know that another name for the Fourth of July was Independence Day?

No question held more interest for me than the distinction between "smart" and "dumb" kids. From early on, teachers made it clear to us that one group faced bright future, the other, a dim one.

I Dream of Jeannie

I rode my fat-tired bicycle the half-mile to Jeannie's house, but walked it beside her all the way back to mine. We had invited her for supper, and my mother was waiting for us at the front door. Right off, she embarrassed me with "I've never seen you walk your bike for anyone before."

I'd been anxious that Jeannie wouldn't go through with it, and, when she did, I was nervous about the food. But if she didn't like hamburgers, corn on the cob, tomatoes from our Victory Garden, and blueberry pie à la mode, I would give up girls forever.

Jeannie Angle was my first date. We were five years old, it was the summer of 1942, and we'd just finished kindergarten. Jeannie had acquired sheets of stamps from Germany, some in denominations of billions of marks from the 1920s, and others bearing Hitler's image from the 1930s. None of us realized that hyper-inflation had made post-World War I Deutschemarks virtually worthless. Nor did we see any connection between the bloated values on the inflation-era stamps and Hitler's rise to power. We just knew we hated Hitler.

Jeannie ate with gusto. When she finished she stood up, lifted her dress above her panties and, beaming with satisfaction, patted her bare stomach. I felt triumphant, accepted. I think it was at that moment that I decided the way to a woman's heart was to feed her. I had been spared, for the time being at least, what I imagined was the ultimate indignity—rejection in love.

War in a Sandbox

For me and my friends, World War II was a game we played in the sandbox. Pearl Harbor was re-enacted hundreds of times because it justified what followed—we fought back and gradually turned the tide. Sandbox wars ended in massive bombing raids on Berlin and Tokyo—the Axis invariably lost because "America controlled the skies."

At school there were air-raid drills, but we regarded the principal's life-and-death exhortations as crying wolf. No "wolves" showed up; no bombs ever fell. After all, didn't we control the skies? On Sunday evenings the family gathered around the radio—which stood on the floor, glowing with an amber-colored light, like a live piece of furniture—to hear Walter Winchell's news bulletin to "all the ships at sea." I loved the hushed intensity in the room as we listened. Churchill's blood, toil, tears, and sweat speech still gives me chills.

The most powerful memories from those years are not events. Pearl Harbor, Hitler's death, and the dropping of the atomic bomb fade when set against the palpable patriotism generated by a common cause. Even kids felt useful. My jobs were to collect old tin cans for repurposing and to help my mother in the Victory Garden and I did both without complaint. The thought of dissenting from this war did not arise. In one voice, we vowed to force our enemies to surrender unconditionally. To us, far from the front, war seemed a game and a good one at that.

World War II ended with a bang when I was nine. Later, my father told me that the Atomic Bomb was like a miniature sun. His attempts to explain its workings interested me less than something new in his voice—awe, tinged with alarm. Throughout the war, he had always sounded confident that things were under control. Now his sober tone warned that nothing would ever be the same. Not long after Hiroshima and Nagasaki, newspapers proclaimed the dawn of the atomic age.

The Travel Bug

Most kids visit their grandparents by car. Not me. Mine lived on the West Coast and to see them my mother, baby brother, and I had twice ridden the train for a week--from New Jersey to Seattle. The first time, I was almost five; the second time, almost nine. We had a roomette to ourselves, but could roam the train under the watchful eyes of "porters," all of whom belonged to The Brotherhood of Sleeping Car Porters, the vanguard union for African-American labor.

As a child I was unaware that blacks were excluded from many Northern towns by gentlemen's agreements that barred them from owning or renting property. Sleeping car porters were the first African-Americans I ever spoke to. Of course, they were not then identified as "African-American," but as "Negroes."

By the time these men had served us a half-dozen breakfasts (of sliced oranges and blueberry pancakes), daily made up our little room, and hovered helpfully from sea to shining sea, they seemed to me like fond uncles. The contrast between the prevailing racist stereotype and my personal experience of these kindly protectors could hardly have been starker. A decade after my first transcontinental journey, when I encountered African-Americans at college, my stereotype-busting experience with the porters helped me bridge what might otherwise have felt like a chasm.

I caught the travel bug early and hard, never losing my lust for exposure to new lands, cultures, foods, and people.

Apprenticeship with a Fact-finder

There aren't many ways a few young children can wreck a house, but we found one. Shelby Leathers, age six, was our leader. She, David Ford, and I—the youngest at five—all lived on Edgewood Road. New houses were going up in our neighborhood. Most were of wood, but this one would be brick. All day we watched as workmen poured the concrete basement and foundation. When they left, Shelby tossed a brick over the edge. Plop it went as it landed below in the wet concrete. Plop, plop, plop. It was soon raining bricks. This was the most fun we'd ever had. We didn't tire till the bricks ran out. Then we went our separate ways.

Somehow my mother found out. She was angrier than I'd ever seen her. The question she asked was, "Why did you do it?" Even a child knows a rhetorical question when he hears one. I knew she meant, "How *could* you have done that!" My Nuremberg defense—Shelby made me—cut no ice with her. She gave me the choice of being spanked by her now or by my father when he got home. I decided to wait and take my chances. She sent me to my room to wait for his return. It felt like death row.

My father got home very late. He and the fathers of my two accomplices had rushed to the scene of the crime, pulled the bricks out one by one as the cement set, and done their best to fill the cavities in the slab. A few more hours and it would have taken jackhammers to remove the bricks, jutting like discolored teeth, from hardened concrete. Postponing my punishment proved to be unwise. The hours of dread made that spanking live forever.

But something unexpected came of the experience. It was my father's line of questioning. He did not ask, "Why did you do it?" What he wanted to know was "What happened?"

I remember this because it was so startling. My mother's questions had filled me with guilt and fear. I had wrecked a house. That was wrong. Therefore, I would be exiled (to my room), shamed, and punished.

My father's questions had the peculiar effect of lifting me out of myself. I almost felt like an onlooker as I described what had happened: we watched the men till they left; then Shelby threw a brick over the side; then David did, and then me. The bricks gurgled as they sunk into the wet cement. When there were no more bricks, we went home. Shelby told us not to tell.

My father completed the story. He told me what he and the other fathers had done to repair the damage, and explained that Shelby, David, and I would be punished to remind us not to do anything like that again.

Both lines of questioning led to the same place—a spanking. My mother's "questions" issued from her moral convictions. My father's questions elicited an exploration of events and consequences—what happened and what followed. The novelty of becoming a witness to my own crime may be why I remember it as if it happened yesterday. My parents' perspectives couldn't have been more different.

That was always my father's question: What happened? Then, what happened next? And after that? The facts, please, all of them. This approach to truth-seeking can be thought of as the scientist's, though actual scientific practice is less formulaic and entails intuitive leaps. To my scientist-father it was second nature. It makes you see yourself from outside, as if you're someone else. It can even lull you into testifying against yourself.

In contrast to my father, my mother hardly seemed to care about the facts. What mattered to her was *doing* what's right (and *not* doing what's wrong).

In later life, she regarded herself as a "Blue Domer," a personal religion without theology, priests, or ritual, where the only authority is oneself, standing under the big blue sky. She claimed that, given half a chance, she would have wrung Hitler's neck. She was married to the same man for over sixty years, but sympathized with her sons' divorces. A housewife who never earned a salary, she volunteered for everything, from the Red Cross to surgeon's assistant at the local hospital, and she won a seat on the school board. She was fierce about equality for women, but paradoxically opposed the Equal Rights Amendment. I think she felt that the ERA represented an insult to the women of her generation whose work, for the most part, had centered on the home.

The point is not the substance of her opinions, but rather the moral certainty with which she held them, and her eager willingness to defend them. Had she been born a generation later, she would have been a general or a statesman in the mold of Margaret Thatcher. In her eighties, from her retirement community in Florida, she helped organize a senior citizens lobby in the state capital. The only thing she ever acknowledged changing her mind about was that the Pope would rule America if a Catholic were elected president.

Where does personal certainty like hers come from? How could it co-exist with my father's focus on fact-finding?

I'd have been a different person if instead of teaching me that the truth is what happened, my parents had personified the view that the truth is what others cannot disprove, or, just as problematic, that the truth is whatever you can get away with. In later years, I watched as leaders engaged in double-talk and their spokesmen maneuvered to preserve deniability. Notions of truth like those are the stock-in-trade of con-artists and spin-doctors. Perhaps nothing we absorb from our elders is more important than their operational definition of truth.

Truth as Synthesis

My family name—Fuller—is one of those English trade names. As Coopers made barrels and Sawyers sawed lumber, Fullers "fulled" cloth. Using internet genealogical tools, the family can be traced back to a William Fuller who lived in Redenhall, England in 1423. Yes, there were Fullers on the Mayflower, but it seems that branch of the family died on the journey to the New World, and that our family is descended from a Thomas Fuller who arrived in 1634.

My father, Calvin Fuller, got a Ph.D. in chemistry from the University of Chicago in 1929. He worked at Bell Laboratory from 1930 until his mandatory retirement at 65 in 1967. During World War II, he served as Synthetic Rubber "czar," travelling by train to inspect production facilities. In 1954, he and two other Bell scientists[2] co-invented the photovoltaic (solar) cell. I remember him demonstrating an early model on our dining room table.

His father, my grandfather, Julius Quincy Fuller, had a drinking problem, which I only learned of when he came to live with us in his sixties. I liked him because he would take me on long walks and tell me about numbers. As an accountant, he was intimate with them, and he liked to play arithmetical games with me. But, in his youth, my father had had to endure his father's drunken tirades and defend his mother from physical abuse.

Now that it's understood that domestic violence tends to pass from one generation to the next, what truly impresses me about my father was that he consciously broke the cycle. He did not pass on to his own family the violence he had experienced as a boy. One of his firmest teachings was that, no matter the provocation, a man *never* strikes a woman. He'd been a victim of violence within his family, but he broke the pattern of passing indignities down the line and instead modeled non-violence for his children.

However, my parents, who both lived into their nineties, were still capable of a vehement argument—with each other, with me and my brothers, and with their peers—right up to the end. The attempt to reconcile their moral and empirical perspectives shaped my life.

Eventually, I came to understand truth as the synthesis sought by the model builder. Building models is what scientists do. They seek explanations that account for all the facts. For scientists the Holy Grail is a theory that reconciles the viewpoints and the findings of all parties.[3]

Synthesis differs from compromise. Compromise is what everyone is willing to settle for, or more simply, what's possible, and indeed compromise is the proper goal of partisan politics.

In contrast, a synthesis has to preserve and combine the essential positions of the parties in a single, consistent framework. The model builder's goal is to explain *all* the data. To this day, I do not feel I've understood something until I can explain it to others.

Truth as Proof

In the third grade we studied the solar system. Our textbook had a diagram of the planets circling the sun. A table gave the distance of each planet from the sun in miles and its period of revolution in days: 365 for the earth, 225 for Venus, just 88 for Mercury, etc. And, printed alongside each planet's orbit, was its average speed in miles per hour.

It was just then that we were learning about circles in arithmetic. The lesson for the week was that the circumference of a circle $C = 2\pi R$, where R is the circle's radius and $\pi = 3.14$ [ad infinitum]. I decided to apply this formula to verify the speed shown in the text for the orbiting earth. The computation was simple enough—just form the product $2\pi R$ and divide by the planet's period in hours.

But something was wrong. My result did not agree with the speed in the book. It was not even close. So I tried the same calculation for Venus and Mercury. No agreement. I did all nine planets. Not one agreed. I did them over and over again. Finally, I asked my father for help. He checked over my figures, looked at the textbook, and announced the unthinkable: the book was wrong. I had thought books couldn't be wrong. We all had.

The next day I showed the error to Mrs. Bahoosian. It made her nervous. She drew me aside and spoke in a conspiratorial whisper. I think she worried that if word got out it might cast doubt on the entire educational enterprise. But she told me that she would write the publishing company.

Months later she told me that the publisher was going to change the numbers in the next edition. She never told the class. I remember checking a year later and, sure enough, the orbits showed my numbers. What a lucky accident the book's figures were wrong! Catching that mistake broke the spell of the printed word, and taught me that the truth is not necessarily what some authority says it is, but rather what can be proven.

When finally found, the truth is common ground on which everyone can stand.

2 | Longing to Belong
(1945–1950)

Volcanic Fame

In fifth grade, I got a taste of fame. Miss Burke was teaching us about volcanoes, and I decided to build one.

I'd been making gunpowder from chemicals my father brought home from Bell Labs. He'd shown me how to mix saltpeter (potassium nitrate), powdered charcoal, and sulfur into an ignitable powder that burned with a flash and released a plume of smoke. Adding powdered magnesium to the mix made the explosion sparkle.

A large flowerpot, turned upside down, gave the volcano a conical shape. Inverted, the hole in the bottom of the pot became the volcano's mouth. Fortified with plaster and rolled in ashes, it looked just like a miniature mountain. Inside went a small stash of gunpowder.

The problem was how to ignite the powder. Reaching under the rim of the volcano with a match ruined the effect. My father suggested that I could set it off remotely by using the transformer that ran my electric train to heat a filament of toaster wire immersed in the charge. The resulting eruption sent sparks and smoke to the ceiling, and filled the classroom with a sulfurous smell.

My volcano was a sensation. I was invited to demonstrate it in every classroom in the school, from my old kindergarten room to the sanctified reaches of the upper grades, where young men and women applauded and demanded encores. The younger kids thought it was magic, the older ones thought it was cool. I discovered that people love explosions.

The recognition my volcano brought me was an eye-opener. Ever since the atomic bomb had brought an end to World War II, physics had seemed glamorous. My father's colleagues at Bell Labs were treated like gods. Einstein was the most famous person on the planet and, for about a week, my classmates regarded me as a wizard. I felt immune to banishment by the Miss Belchers of the world. At last, my place was secure. Some of my classmates were not so fortunate.

Gerald

Gerald stands out because from our first sums in kindergarten to high school algebra the two of us competed in mathematics. For more than a decade we were like tennis rivals who improve each other's game.

Gerald's parents owned a chicken farm. They had left Germany before the war. Gerald hated Hitler like the rest of us, but insisted that not all Germans were bad. I would ride five miles on my bicycle to visit him on his chicken farm and sometimes his mother invited me to stay for supper. Although his parents spoke English with a German accent, like Nazis in the movies, they seemed okay to me. Their shame over their native country provided a glimpse of the power of cultural identity.

Although we were peers in math, Gerald's and my prospects were hardly equal. Growing up, it had always been assumed that I would go to college and graduate school, and so I did. Gerald was expected to sell the eggs produced on the farm, and ended up driving a truck that supplied supermarkets.

At a high school reunion in our sixties, I asked Gerald whether he regretted not developing his talent for math. There were several of us gathered around and everyone present remembered our old rivalry. With an unmistakable wistfulness, Gerald explained that his parents had assumed he'd take over the farm. None of his teachers had encouraged him to pursue his talent.

Learning from Failure

Burt was two years older than the rest of us and at age eleven that made a big difference. He was a man to us boys and he would demonstrate his supremacy by beating us up one at a time. With fearful regularity he'd single out a fresh victim and start a fight, which he invariably ended by administering a "pink-belly"—rapid, repetitive slapping of our bellies, like bongo drums, until they turned pink.

Fed up with this, I pulled ten of his serial victims aside and persuaded them to jump him, all together, the next time he picked on any one of us. In a film, I'd seen the classic demonstration of the collective strength of breakable sticks when enough of them are bundled together, and I fancied that the message of strength through unity would be self-evident.

Handing a slender stick to each of my friends, I told them to think of themselves as the sticks. I asked one of the boys for his stick and broke it over my knee to show them what Burt was doing to us by taking us on one at a time. Then, collecting a stick from each boy and tying them into a bundle, I passed it around the circle. Try breaking it now, I said in the confident voice I recalled from the film. The bundle had the girth of a two-by-four and the point was made, though several of the boys gave it a try. I took their grim expressions and solemn nods to mean that we'd confront Burt as one.

The next day Burt picked a fight with Tom. I shouted the agreed-upon signal and jumped on Burt's back. As he tried to shake me off, I pictured the other boys piling on and bringing him down. A moment later Tom and I were on the ground, our faces in the dirt. Having two enemies inspired Burt to deal with us both more harshly than he would have dealt with either of us alone.

Our friends had hung back for a few fateful seconds, waiting to see how things would go. Then, humbled and ashamed, they scurried off as Burt called after them, "You're next, chickens!"

The moral, which I grasped years later, was that an abstract strategy, albeit sound, must be practiced until it can be executed perfectly, even under stress. When strength is sought in numbers, organization and timing are everything. As the Labor Movement showed, exploited individuals can combine forces to level the playing field. Nothing new in this, of course. But like many before me, I only learned the operational complexities of *E pluribus unum* from failure.

The Bridge of Music

I didn't sing with the other kids. From kindergarten on, I just stood by, embarrassed, as the teacher played the piano and my classmates raised their voices in song. I think the idea of joining in threatened what must have been a precarious sense of individuality. While I sought belonging, I also feared too much of it. Or, it may have been that when I pictured myself in song, I felt ridiculous. (I still do.) For whatever reason, I did not sing then and only pretend to now.

The seventh grade teacher was the first to notice this and one day he offered to help me overcome what he interpreted as shyness. It was agreed that instead of joining the other kids on the playground after lunch, I would meet him in our classroom. I was secretly excited by this opportunity. I thought that if I could join my friends in song, I might cease to feel like a witness to my own life and lose myself in the group. But, as Mr. Finelli led me to the piano, he got a call from the principal's office and had to step out. As he left, he said we'd have our session within a few days, but, alas, my private tutorial never again reached the top of his agenda.

It was around this time that I persuaded my mother to buy an old piano. If I couldn't sing, maybe I could make a place for myself by playing the piano, while others gathered round and did the singing. Two of my classmates, Linda Kennedy and Lucia Taylor, already played and they were both very popular. The piano seemed to offer a way out of solitary, one that didn't require total merging. To me, it provided a solution to the quandary of achieving togetherness while maintaining separation.

Our second-hand upright player piano cost fifty dollars, and fit into a corner of the living room next to the little wall clock that governed the duration of my practices. Mrs. Smith, who played the organ in a local church, was engaged to give me weekly lessons at two dollars each. She started me out on scales and soon moved to simple hymns. When I brought sheet music of popular hits she incorporated them into the lessons. No matter how egregious my rendition of a new piece, her suggestions invariably began with the words, "Bobby, you have a slight tendency to...." It became a family joke. I'd say to my brother, "Steve, you have a slight tendency to eat like a pig." Or our mother would say, "Boys, your rooms are showing a slight tendency toward chaos."

Within a few years I could play Christmas carols and popular tunes from the Hit Parade. At school dances, Linda or Lucia and I would perform duets. Our classmates greeted the announcement that we were about to perform with polite applause, but once we'd gotten past the first few bars, the piano was drowned out by their chatter. This left me with a lifelong sympathy for musicians who perform in bars and restaurants.

The piano never delivered on its promise to subdue my witness, but it did open up a channel of communication with Linda Kennedy. I used it like an enigma machine to encrypt my first love letter.

In seventh grade I handed Linda a coded message:

ceaacbagfedce,dfbbcg.ceaacbagfedce,dfbbcc.cbagfgabbb;cbagfgaddd.

Soon, I got a line of code back:

ggggggagec,ddddddedb.ccccdeffffgabcbaged.

Racing to the nearest piano, I plunked away at the keyboard until I realized that she had responded to the notes of *If I Loved You* from *Carousel* with *A Wonderful Guy* from *South Pacific*.

3 | Becoming
(1950–1952)

Les Misérables

That is part of the beauty of all literature. You discover that your long-ings are universal longings, that you're not lonely and isolated from any-one. You belong.

– F. Scott Fitzgerald

In 1950, as our little band moved on to high school, our attention focused on the new bodies appearing in place of those we'd known since kindergarten. In my fourteenth year, I grew almost a foot. About this time I became aware of a serious undercurrent of competitiveness. This was a natural outgrowth of childhood games, but now we ourselves were the winners and losers, not the stand-in toy soldiers we'd deployed in our sandboxes.

Though physical fights were rare, relations between us were becoming a kind of covert war. Lives were not at stake, but reputations were. Competition assumed many forms—sports, grades, clothes, popularity, and dates. In these contests, we were forging provisional identities. Lucia was a cheerleader, destined for prom queen; Tom, the class clown, destined for Harvard; and David, a three-letter varsity athlete harboring a mental illness that, in time, would cause him to take his own life.

Of course, competition had actually been there from the beginning. In third grade we'd all had to come up to bat as the teacher presented a problem in arithmetic: "Sandra, step up to the plate. Are you ready? Here's the pitch: 3 times 4." If Sandra replied with 12 she went to first base, which was a flowerpot by the windows. If she got it wrong, it was strike one. It was fun for the good "hitters," but for those who regularly struck out it was even more humiliating than doing so on the playground.

High school sports were like medieval jousting with ladies cheering on their knights and wearing their colors. If a boy didn't compete in sports, his best strategy for getting a girlfriend was to acquire a car. But there was nothing like playing on a varsity team when it came to social success. As boys prized looks in girls, girls valued status in boys, and this heightened the competition among us. It was an unwritten rule that only suitors of high status should ask the prettiest girls out.

The importance of status for males and beauty for females made many young lives miserable. Everyone took it for granted that rank and looks determined your options.

A less reliable route to recognition was grades. High grades did not equate with broad popularity, but in certain circles academic success was valued, and competition for grades was fierce. I'd study many extra hours in the hope of outscoring my classmates by even a point or two. Though my father encouraged academic excellence, he was skeptical of spending so much effort on such marginal returns. He argued that there were more important things to learn than the conjugation of a few more obscure Latin verbs. I knew he was right. I was on the cusp of realizing that without this competitive element—and the status it earned me in the eyes of a particular girl whom I hoped to impress—much of my motivation would evaporate. What kept me at it was that the Latin teacher, Mr. Lynch, returned our exams in the order of our scores: highest grade first, second highest second, and so on, down to Forrest Collier who invariably received his exam last. Winning was rewarded with public honor, losing with disgrace. My incentive was to outscore and impress Judy, who was always among the top three.

My principal adversary in this, and just about everything else, was Jim Edgar. In basketball Jim—who was taller, stronger, and a better rebounder—beat me out for starting center. I could accept losing the position to him, but hated its implications in the realm of romance. He and Judy were soon going steady. In my melancholy, I made friends with the moon.

Freshman year, we were required to read a novel of our choosing. In one of those seeming accidents that change lives, Mr. Champlin, the English teacher who doubled as baseball coach, urged me to read a book by a French writer named Victor Hugo. It was *Les Misérables*. The teacher was so set on this that he personally withdrew the book from the school library and placed it in my hands. Its title didn't bode well, and its heft was daunting.

Shoveling snow had shown me that the largest tasks can be accomplished if broken up into small ones. I set myself the goal of plowing through *Les Misérables*, one chapter a day.

When the bishop covered for Jean Valjean by telling the police that the silver Valjean had stolen from the rectory was a gift, I was hooked. No book has ever had a more powerful impact on me.

Hugo's title applied equally to his characters and to my classmates. Although I was passing as a somebody, I felt like a nobody, and I identified with the *misérables* in my class. I wanted to understand the private world of Forrest, hopeless at Latin but the architect of a basement-wide railway for his model trains; of Douglas, who was already hand-crafting his first of many pipe organs; of short, stocky Ronald—in love with Carol, the most beautiful girl in the school—reading aloud the love letters he wrote her; of Carol herself, who reportedly gave peep shows for boys perched in trees outside her bedroom; of Chuck with whom I discovered the beauty and power of calculus as revealed in the paperback *A Mathematician's Delight*; of Jim, in whom science and Christian fundamentalism cohabited harmoniously; of Donald, whom I tutored in English vocabulary[4]; of Noel Hinners, later a top administrator at NASA, who gave me a bird's-eye view of New Jersey from his Piper Cub; of Fred, who shot dead his girlfriend's father for forbidding him to date his daughter; of Pamela, initiating, in rapid succession, four of my classmates into the mysteries of sex on the pool table in the basement of the Presbyterian Church. At graduation she famously inscribed their yearbooks, "As you go through life, try to take some of the weight on your elbows."

Jimmy would have been in our class but he suffered from Down Syndrome and spent his days wandering forlornly around town, the target of merciless ridicule. Everyone knew him as "Jimmy the Nut." His round, ruddy face was usually tear-stained. He fascinated me, but when I tried to talk to him, he turned and ran, only to stop and resume his plaintive vigil from a distance.

I've known Tom Purvis since kindergarten. In the 1940s, we began what would become a series of Christmas Eve walks that continues to this day. In high school, Tom was an Ichabod Crane-like figure, very tall and ridiculously thin, who shielded himself from ribbing by playing the clown.

While Tom Purvis found a way to survive ridicule, and went on to a career in government, his chubby neighbor Tommy suffered irreversible damage. Tommy never left his childhood home. The last time anyone saw him, shortly before he died at fifty, he was miserable, obese, and house-bound. As the world is now coming to realize, bullying can be fatal.

The physical world interested me, but not nearly as much as my classmates and their problems. Though my questions evolved as I matured, the origins of my various adult identities can all be found in sophomoric questions that took root in school.

The Power of Lists

My father taught me how to make money, how to save it, and how to invest. He even gave me my first paying job: mowing our lawn, once a week during the growing season, for two dollars a pop. Within a month, I was pushing our old hand mower over the lawns of a half-dozen neighbors. During my second summer, I put all my savings into the purchase of a Toro power mower and took on another half-dozen lawns. With the Toro I had to take special care to avoid stones and fresh dog poop, which the mower expelled, respectively, as deadly projectiles and noxious mists.

By my fourth and final year in the business, I had two power mowers, and guided them simultaneously, one with each hand, over the twenty lawns in my grassy empire. Most noteworthy of my clients was Walter Brattain, my father's colleague at Bell Labs, who won the Nobel Prize for having co-invented the transistor. Getting to know "Mr. Brattain" as a teenager was one reason that, when later in life I met other Nobel Laureates, I didn't regard the prize as obligating me to treat them as deities. Though Brattain was not immune to vainglory, he knew that, in spite of his success, he was an ordinary person, and he let me in on the secret.

My father's mentoring included not just the mechanics of mowing lawns, but, significantly, the maintenance of the tools of the trade and, still more important, the records of work done.

I kept lists of all my customers, the dates when I mowed their lawns, whether or not my agreement included trimming (something I tried to avoid because it took a disproportionate amount of time and cut into hourly earnings), and, finally, a record of payments received. I kept track of finances to the penny and totaled up my net worth at least once a week. Though my total wealth rarely exceeded a few hundred dollars, it seemed like a fortune.

One day while mowing the Rothenburger's lawn, I was pondering the things I wanted to see happen in my life—get an A in English, ask Judy for a date, win the piano competition for high school orchestra, and be a starter on the junior varsity basketball team. When the items reached six in number, I felt I was losing track and that if I didn't put my full attention on each goal, some would never be realized. In that moment, it occurred to me to put the tasks swirling in my head onto a single list and *work the list*, checking daily on each one, until they were all accomplished.

I can't explain why such a simple idea felt so revelatory. I went home and made the first of what would be a lifetime of To Do Lists. By the time I left high school the following year I'd checked off all my original entries and had a new list. Later, at my various jobs, I kept lists of the balls I had in the air. As a writer, working lists of agents, editors, publishers, and blurbers makes rejections easier to handle. When one turns you down, you simply cross the name off your list and add another.

A Speck in the Cosmos

At thirteen, I put all my lawn-mowing profits into a roundtrip train ticket to visit Billy Dickinson—my former classmate and teammate—who, upon graduating from eighth grade, had moved with his parents to Albuquerque, New Mexico. Traveling with my mother across America in a private compartment was no preparation for sitting up for three nights in coach on my own.

A soldier in uniform, who had the seat beside me, befriended me with the offer of a Coke, and then, when the lights dimmed for the night, attempted to parlay his offering into permission to molest me. As I felt his hand creeping across my leg, I excused myself, and locked myself in a men's room for the night, returning only as the train arrived at its destination where I figured I could safely disembark in the company of the other passengers. The memory that endures is less of my initial shock than the stink of the men's room and the anguished look on the young soldier's face as he whispered an apology and begged me not to tell. I didn't tell, but I didn't forget either.

Billy and I spent a month swimming, riding horses, and shooting his BB gun at anything that moved on the desert floor. On the train, I'd begun making an outline of the history of the ancient world based on a library book I'd borrowed for the summer. When Billy badgered me to come out and play, I'd insist on first completing a summary of the day's readings of the life of the Egyptians, Babylonians, Assyrians, Hebrews, Persians, or (my favorite) the Phoenicians.

Billy's parents were evangelical Christians and they never gave up hope of recruiting me into their church. While the Golden Rule and Sermon on the Mount intrigued me, Mildred and Clarence were upset that I gave equal time to studying the heathens in my book of ancient history. From my first exposure, the history of the ancients and the archeology of our hominid ancestors has done for me what religious faith does for people like the Dickinsons: provided access to feelings of humility and wonder. Paradoxically, an occasional glimpse of oneself as a speck in the cosmos helps to surmount the inhibitions that prevent us from taking a stand. After all, what's there to lose?

Teen Epiphany—Beyond Belief

Know you what it is to be a child? ...it is to believe in belief....

– Francis Thompson, British poet

We don't forget our first epiphany any more than we forget our first kiss. The difference is we know what a kiss is, but don't know what to make of a stroke of illumination. The experience lingers in memory as something special, but since we can't place it, we keep it to ourselves.

Only years later did I realize that an Ah-ha experience I'd had in my teens was the philosophical counterpart of that first kiss. One day it struck me that there were no final truths, no ultimate explanations. I shared my experience of unbelief with no one at the time, knowing that I couldn't explain myself and fearing others' mockery.

In science courses I'd noticed that the chain of assumptions upon which theories rested always ended in other assumptions. I accepted grounding scientific theories in hypotheses—it didn't seem to undercut their usefulness. But I still wanted to believe there were absolute, unimpeachable moral truths. My mother certainly acted as if there were.

But not long after my realization about scientific theories, I had the premonition that this same principle applied to beliefs of every sort—scientific, political, moral, or personal. How, exactly, could beliefs be demonstrated with absolute certainty, I wondered. It seemed to me that any belief could be challenged and might need qualification in certain circumstances.

It was like the feeling, when consulting a dictionary, that there are no final definitions, only cross-references. I remember standing alone in my bedroom when this hit me. It was sobering, yet at the same time, strangely liberating. Until then I'd believed that final explanations and ultimate truths existed and it behooved us to know what they were and to conform.

With this revelation, my hopes for unambiguous solutions to life's problems dimmed. From that moment on, I would be on my own.

I decided that to function in society I would have to pretend to go along with the prevailing consensus that certain beliefs were self-evident—at least until I could come up with something better. For decades afterwards, without understanding why, I was drawn to people and ideas that expanded my foretaste of a world built not on absolute, infallible beliefs, but on falsifiable, provisional assumptions.

Experiment with Identity

About the middle of my sophomore year in high school, my mother saw a story in the paper about an experimental early-admissions program to college. To find out if the last year or two of high school were superfluous, the Ford Foundation was offering college scholarships to qualified sophomores and juniors willing to serve as guinea pigs. You had to take an SAT-like aptitude test and submit your high school record.

I told my mother I wasn't interested. I'd lived all my fifteen years in the same little town, loved my friends, and was satisfied with my life. My mother said, "Just take the test. It'll be good practice for later. If you get in, you can always turn them down."

Months after taking the test, during which I'd not thought once about college, a fat envelope arrived from Oberlin offering admission. I put the packet on the mantel and circled it warily for about a month, struggling with the decision of what to do. I could have said no. Neither parent pressured me to accept Oberlin's offer. Leaving high school would mean giving up a safe, familiar game for an uncertain one. It would not mean giving up sports glory, because there was no glory for second-stringers like me anyway. But it would mean giving up the position of pianist in the high school orchestra and the ceremonial role of president of the junior class, to which I had been elected by my classmates.

SpongeBob

There's not much the winner of an election can say about *why* he won that doesn't come across as a brag. But, with your indulgence, and because this event illuminates others of which I will tell, I'm going to pause long enough in the narrative to suggest an explanation.

My opponent was none other than Jim Edgar, basketball star, "A" student, Judy's boyfriend, your quintessential BMOC (Big Man On Campus).

I'd never have chosen to run against him, but somehow I was nominated. There was no campaigning, and, as everyone admired Jim, I resigned myself to losing in a landslide. I felt obliged to vote for him myself as he'd beaten me in the two things I cared most about—basketball and love. When the votes were counted, Jim had about twenty and I had over one hundred.

Although I was initially astonished by the outcome, it did not take long to understand what had happened. While everyone greeted Jim in the halls between classes, and felt thrilled if he reciprocated, I had a different kind of relationship with my classmates. I knew many of them intimately. I'd been in their homes, met their families, helped some with math, and spent hours inquiring into their lives. I knew their hobbies, their sorrows, and their secret loves.

Lest you get the impression that I was only interested in the lives of nobodies, I should add that I knew Jim and most of the other somebodies in this same way.

So why the win? Because there are a lot more nobodies than somebodies and Jim mostly hung out with the somebodies. What I had stumbled upon in winning the election was the power of recognition. Getting to know how my classmates ticked filled a hole in my soul. That listening to them might lead to a leadership role had never crossed my mind.

Delving into others' lives taught me that although most of my classmates were not regarded as somebodies, they were hardly the nobodies they were taken for. On the contrary, their private lives were as rich as those of the class celebrities. You could say that this was the other side of the discovery that my Nobel-prize winning neighbor, Walter Brattain, was not just a somebody, he was also an approachable, fascinating person quite apart from his celebrity.

Later in life, my interest in others led one critic to dub me an "ontological vampire." A bit harsh perhaps, if blood-sucker is what comes to mind, but I could not deny that all my life I have found nourishment in absorbing the lives of others. Call me "SpongeBob."[5]

Taking the Leap

Leap and a net will appear.
– John Burroughs

I may have decided to accept Oberlin's offer because boredom was a greater threat to me than failure. Or, it may have been that I was beginning to realize that I would not find answers to my questions where I was, and that I might elsewhere. Slowly, but ineluctably, the idea of being a guinea pig at Oberlin had begun to grow on me. A rising inner voice said, *you can't say no to this.*

My decision to go also fit a pattern of diving in over my head and surviving. When I was about three, my parents took me out in a rowboat on Chesapeake Bay and the waves made me seasick. My mother told me either to stop whining or get out. I couldn't imagine anything worse than that boat, so I climbed over the side. She grabbed my hand and trailed me along in the water, but wouldn't help me back into the boat until I promised to behave. When I finally agreed to her terms and she hauled me in, the seasickness was gone.

So it happened that in the Fall of 1952, with my bicycle tied to the roof of our Chevy, my parents drove me to Ohio. As my father left, he presented me a little notebook he had titled *Pointers.* Inside, in his own hand, were sections on manners, morals, learning, love—everything a boy should know. My mother gave me a tin of homemade cookies. I was on my own with only my bicycle for companion—and within a few weeks, it had been stolen.

4 | Belonging
(1952–1955)

Surfacing

By the end of my first month at Oberlin, I realized that I'd leapt into an abyss. For the next two months I was in free fall. The identity I'd brought with me from high school didn't work in college. My roommate argued that my scientific perspective was mechanistic, reductive, and anti-humanistic. A dormitory mate, who saw himself as a literary lion, treated me with condescension verging on disdain. I tried modeling myself after a cool older student whom I admired, but the identity transplant didn't take.

The French professor said I spoke the language as though my mouth were full of potatoes. Even I could sense that my English composition was adolescent. The biology professor lectured for an hour on the enzymes in the frog and on the next exam, expected us to name them all. The only reassurance I got that semester was that two days of private tutorial by Professor Fuzzy Vance were enough to close the math gap left by skipping junior and senior year.

The expectations of my college professors rudely ended the delusions of competence I'd acquired in high school. By Thanksgiving I had begun to suspect that I would drown. As Christmas break approached, I decided to do everything conceivable to prepare for a biology test and see if that made a difference. If memorization was what was required, then I'd memorize everything that might possibly be asked. In high school I'd usually been able to tell how I'd done on a test the minute it was over, but this time I wasn't so sure.

I awaited the verdict with resignation. I had the unfamiliar feeling that my fate was out of my hands. But no matter how things turned out it would be okay, because if doing everything I could think of wasn't enough, then this game was not for me.

In going to Oberlin I'd unwittingly jettisoned an identity in which my dignity was secure. Now I wondered if I would ever feel that I belonged anywhere. The answer came to me at home over Christmas break in the self-addressed envelope I'd left with the biology professor. I'd given him what he wanted, and he'd given me an "A." But the experience of taking exams that required rote memorization had sown seeds of discontent that would grow until they changed the direction of my life.

The 1950s—my college years—were those of the Red Scare and Senator Joseph McCarthy's witch-hunts. Oberlin students crowded around the one tiny television in the snack bar. My class showed its collective contempt for McCarthy by electing Boris Oblesov, a Russian immigrant, class president.

One of my closest friends was a math student named Judd Fermi. A rumor circulated in the dorm that Judd's father had built the atom bomb. Indeed, Enrico Fermi had built the first nuclear reactor, he was a key player in the wartime Manhattan Project to build the Bomb, and he remains one of the most important figures in twentieth century physics. Judd claimed that as a child he'd believed his father's story that the goal of the secret work in Los Alamos was to design windshield wipers for submarines.

Judd had his father's talent for mathematics and physics. His way of sizing up math problems was a revelation to me: abstract, from outside the problem's particulars; mine was computational, formulaic, pedestrian. Gradually, by hanging out with him, I absorbed some of his mathematical sophistication. My relationship with Judd was one of many apprenticeships through which I would acquire my real education.

Another classmate was an African from a place few of us had heard of—the Portuguese colony of Mozambique in Southeast Africa. Drinking coffee in the snack bar with Judd and me, Eduardo Mondlane described his plans to drive the Portuguese rulers out of his country and build an independent nation. That sounded dangerous to me and I recall warning Eduardo (as if he didn't know!) that he might get himself killed.

After graduating from Oberlin and marrying a classmate, Mondlane founded FRELIMO, the leading party in his country's revolution. He was assassinated during the struggle, but today is regarded as the George Washington of Mozambique. Despite Mozambique's colonial and racist history, Eduardo had nothing against white people. Indeed, his wife was white. His colorblind vision of justice anticipated Nelson Mandela's. His nation-building vision showed me that it's okay to think big.

Oberlin College was proud of its admissions policy. Since its founding in 1833, the College had taken all qualified applicants regardless of sex, race, class, religion, or national origin. Oberlin's was the classic liberal political philosophy, and one consequence was that until the 1960s, nearly half of all blacks who graduated from predominately white American colleges came from that one school.

It was at Oberlin that I first got to know an African-American. Bill Cline could beat anyone in the state in the quarter-mile sprint. I never missed his races. It didn't seem to affect him that the stands were empty at track meets. Cline was not beguiled by glamour. His speed dazzled, but what intrigued me most was that he did not need an audience; he ran for himself. Twenty years later, I would emulate him and discover the sheer exhilaration of running with speed and power. When your fellow humans are withholding recognition, there can be reassurance and solace in training your body to do something well.

Life in a Test Tube?

A question Judd and I shared was whether life could be produced in a test tube. A few of us would-be scientists debated this with the religious humanists, a group led by my roommate David Thomas. Is life a potential property of matter or does it require something more? Why shouldn't the rules of physics and chemistry apply to the molecular constituents of living things?

Judd and I argued that all you had to do was get the right combination of chemicals together in the right environment and presto, Life would begin, evolution would take over, and a few billion years later people would be walking around, even college students—like us!

Dave and his allies held that there could be no Life without a divine spark. We tried to depict them as rearguing the Scopes monkey trial, and fancied ourselves Clarence Darrow. They dismissed us, with condescension that rivaled our own, as callous mechanists, profaning the sacred. I wonder how it would have affected our discussions if we'd been aware that, while we were arguing, Francis Crick and James Watson had deciphered the genetic code.

Judd subsequently made a career in Cambridge, England studying the molecular structure of life-supporting compounds like hemoglobin. My stake in the debate grew out of a personal quandary which could be traced to my foundation-wrecking escapade. In my view, producing life in a test tube was a challenge that science would eventually have to meet if it were to claim to have a final, convincing theory of everything, an understanding so comprehensive and persuasive that it could settle all arguments (even those between my parents and me). Something inclusive that would close the apparent gap between the evidence-based causal laws of science and the faith-based laws of morality, that is, the epistemological gap between my father and my mother. It seemed to me that for such a program to have a chance, there could be no unbridgeable difference between animate and inanimate matter. In other words, it should be possible to make life in the laboratory. I spent my sophomore and junior years concentrating on math and physics courses, hoping someday to advance this agenda.[6]

It never occurred to me then that even if life were created in the laboratory, the God question would not thereby be settled—not in the minds of true believers anyway. They could always argue that God had been hovering over the biochemists and, just as they combined all the necessary ingredients, had waved His wand to bring inert matter to life. Or, with greater sophistication, they could argue that God was not an external agent, necessary to spark life, but rather that life is a self-emergent property arising in complex molecules, and preserve a role for God as the author of the natural laws governing the process.

Granted, this would not be the personal God whom believers petition in their prayers, but it would avoid jettisoning God completely. Many scientists make no distinction between God and the underlying physical principles—some understood, some not—that account for natural phenomena. Einstein, for one, said that he believed in "Spinoza's God who reveals himself in the orderly harmony of what exists, not in a God who concerns himself with the fates and actions of human beings."[7]

Accidental Education

...accidental education, whatever its economical return... was prodigiously successful as an object in itself.

– Henry Adams, *The Education of Henry Adams*

How often a seemingly accidental experience marks a turning point in our lives—a point where a curtain drops and a new vista opens. With an all important calculus test scheduled two days hence, a classmate, Pete Radcliffe, mentioned that he was hitchhiking to Toledo that afternoon to see a traveling Van Gogh exhibit. Radcliffe was class valedictorian and a legendary free-spirit who, in a dramatic stunt, had ridden a white horse across the campus urging everyone to see Marlon Brando in the title role in *Viva Zapata* at the local theater. Pete invited me to go with him to Toledo, and he overcame my predisposition to over-prepare for exams by arguing that we'd be back in time to brush up.

This was a chance to break the stranglehold of a rigid scholastic ideal and add a wild card to my learning strategy. Nervous, but egged on by Pete to stop playing it safe, I agreed to go. It wasn't *what* we saw, it was *that* I went that made the difference.

In retrospect, my mother came to regret her part in the Oberlin experiment. She wished I'd finished high school, gone to an Ivy League college, and stuck with one job for life, like my father. She believed that in not finishing high school I established a pattern of not finishing anything. But I think the Ford Foundation was on to something. There were a few dozen of us guinea pigs at Oberlin, and by spring semester none of us felt we'd missed out on anything.

A brush with failure is something that you never consciously choose, and that changes you whether you survive or not. Had I not been faced with a sink-or-swim situation at fifteen, and found my way back to the surface, I doubt I'd have been game for subsequent dives. Measured against my mother's expectations—one job, one spouse—leaving high school early *was* a mistake. But in that first fateful leap, I learned to notice when circumstances were separating me from my passion, and I gained enough confidence to trust my instincts, opt out, and start over.

Déjà Vu, Exit Two

For most of my first semester at Oberlin about all I'd done right was to carry a clean handkerchief. When, just prior to Christmas break, I caught on and things began to go better, I forgot my initial difficulties and completed most of what the College had to offer in math and physics in a few years. Toward the end of my junior year I began to experience *déjà vu*. Though there were entire fields of knowledge I'd not even touched at that point, I didn't then want to do anything but science. And in science, I felt further progress at Oberlin was unlikely. Instead of going to classes, I was spending a lot of time flying around the country in a small plane that a friend of mine had put together from spare parts. Students were forbidden to have cars at Oberlin, but there was no prohibition against planes. So Tony Newcomb had built one in a barn on the edge of town.

We began with short flights over the College, but soon we were flying up and down the East Coast. Although we had a few close calls—due primarily to not landing before our destination was shrouded in darkness—we never crashed. It was probably fortunate that I didn't spend a fourth year at

Oberlin, because our luck might not have held. In any case, by the middle of my junior year, the thought of moving on, as I had done in high school, had crept into my mind.

My parents held a cocktail party that Christmas for my father's colleagues at Bell Labs. Home from college and eighteen, I was old enough to mingle with the guests. The vice-president for research at Bell asked about my plans for graduate school and I told him I could hardly wait. He told me the best physics department in the country was his alma mater Princeton and suggested that I visit its physics department over the holiday break. When I reminded him that I was just a junior and had a year to go before graduation, he brushed that aside as of no account. I didn't fully recognize what was happening, but even then I had the sense that I had been taken under his wing. Later I would understand that, at that party, as the eldest son of my father, recently honored for co-inventing the solar cell, I had become the unwitting beneficiary of an influential and powerful old boys' network.

A few days after Christmas, I got a call from Princeton informing me that I had an appointment with the dean of the graduate school. Driving the forty miles from Chatham to Princeton, I had a premonition that my life was again about to change. After a brief interview with the dean, I was taken to the physics building where I was introduced to several professors.

To my astonishment, they seemed to be courting me! No one mentioned the absence of a college degree. At the end of the day, I left with an application in hand, and when I got back to Oberlin, I filled it out and sent it in. But none of that really mattered. What counted was that I was Calvin Fuller's son and the Vice President for Research at Bell Labs had put in a word for me with his buddies at Princeton.

That spring I received a letter offering me one of a few dozen coveted positions as a first year physics student at Princeton for the academic year 1955–56. Like all offers of admission to the graduate school, it included financial support in the form of a research assistantship. Although I knew I'd been the beneficiary of favoritism, I didn't even consider letting such scruples prevent me from taking the yellow brick road that now lay open before me. When you're young and sought after, it's easy to ignore the tiny voice in your head that knows you better than those courting you and has doubts about your deservedness and capabilities.

When I told Judd Fermi what had happened, he phoned his father, Enrico, and the next day Judd learned that there was a spot for him in Princeton's math department. Judd's father was among the most esteemed physicists in the world and a wartime colleague of several of the professors at Princeton. Whereas it had taken me a few months to get into Princeton, a place was found for Judd within hours. What's more important, Judd was intellectually mature enough to do graduate work. I was not so sure about myself.

I had come to Oberlin with two big questions, one intellectual and one personal. The first was the life-in-a-test-tube question, a precursor of my more abstract question as to whether morality and causality were governed by distinct, independent set of laws. On the answer to that question depended the possibility of reconciling religion and science and, in personal terms, reaching agreement between me and my college critics.

Undeterred by my failure to convince my roommate and his fellow humanists, I plunged ahead determined to see if mathematics, biology, chemistry, and physics could, at least in principle, be brought to bear on moral questions.

Should that program fail, at least physics and mathematics promised certainty within their own domains. From the start, I had found math's certainties to be an impregnable fortress against the shame of being wrong. In math I could prove I was right, and no one, not even my mother, would be able to find fault.

And then there was the personal and increasingly urgent question—the obsession of most young men—can I get a girl? Can I find someone to stand with me against the uncaring world?

For the first two years at Oberlin, I was, as in high school, too timid to ask for a date. It would be easy to blame my shyness on my age since I was younger than most, but I was also taller, and that lucky circumstance had concealed my true age to all but a few intimates. No, what held me back was the fear of rejection.

Finally, halfway through my third and final year at Oberlin, a senior chemistry major, Mary Alice, took me under her tutelage and introduced me to the mysteries of love, all except the ultimate one. Another senior, a headstrong philosophy major named Ruth was more adventurous. That fall, her fiancé had died of heart failure and she was suddenly alone. Ruth had short platinum hair and a fierce, independent streak. She suggested we hitchhike to Niagara Falls over a long weekend. There, where many before me had honeymooned, so did I.

These young women, four years my senior, completed my sentimental education, providing an eye-opening initiation into the catalytic power of eros. My tutors in love were about to graduate, which made my own exit all the more desirable. In May 1955, I packed up my things and left Oberlin College, glad to be putting an end to that chapter of my life.

5 | Banishment
(1955–1957)

Number-Crunching

I spent the summer of 1955 before enrolling at Princeton as a research assistant at Bell Labs. Every weekday I rode with my father in a carpool of scientists who worked at Bell. It was exciting to lunch with people whose names were in physics texts and the newspapers.[8] I noticed immediately that no matter how famous they were, they treated each other with respect, even extending it to me and the other summer intern, a third year Princeton graduate student.[9] The easy-going collegiality, the tacit humility before Nature, and the devotion to understanding and applying natural law defined the company culture. No academic institution I've ever worked in has been as devoid of one-upmanship, as free of elitism, as Bell Labs in the fifties.[10]

I was presented with several project alternatives at Bell, and chose to work with Dr. David Rose (whose easygoing nature I connected with his being the father of triplets). He gave me the task of performing calculations for a project that today I remember little of except that the equations were immensely long and complicated and we were soon forced to use an early electronic computer in the attempt to solve them.

In 1955, there were only a few computers in the world, and access to them was strictly rationed. Bell Lab's machine was the size of a small house and you fed it data on punch cards, which it digested for hours before regurgitating answers, most of which were manifestly wrong. That was because its circuits consisted not of transistors but of vacuum tubes, which had a tendency to burn out in the middle of long computations, thereby rendering hours of number-crunching useless. The low priority given to my project meant that I only got to use the machine between midnight and daybreak, and the unreliable vacuum tubes meant that many of those lonely nights bore no fruit at all. The summer was over before the equations were reliably solved, and I was relieved to be off to Princeton.

Valhalla—In the Hall of the Gods

The physics department at Princeton saw itself as the center of the intelligent universe. This conceit was not based on the fact that Einstein had spent his last twenty years at Princeton's Institute for Advanced Study, but his longtime proximity to the university certainly lent credibility to the claim. The great man had died months before my arrival, and more advanced graduate students, who had been to his house for tea, would describe their meetings with him in reverential tones. Most of them, that is, for even then there were some who tried to make themselves look important by badmouthing his solitary and unsuccessful quest for a theory that unified gravitation and electromagnetism.

Every afternoon at four o'clock, tea and cookies were served in an oak-paneled room in Fine Hall. Stained-glass windows, emblazoned with Einstein's law of gravitation and Heisenberg's uncertainty principle, graced one wall. In attendance were some of the very men whose theories we were learning—scientists who already had Nobel prizes, and, as it turned out, many more who would eventually be so honored. This was Valhalla.

These scientists knew how nuclear weapons worked; they had built them. While they were working on the Manhattan Project at Los Alamos, I had been in fifth grade showing off my volcano. Now they were teaching us nuclear physics, barely concealing their delight in the technical elegance of the Bomb. With such information growing inside me, I sensed an impasse. On the one hand, I was glad that this extraordinary energy resided in the nucleus and that it was our side that had first teased it out. I took it for granted that World War II had to be fought and won. But now the Soviet Union seemed committed to spreading its communist doctrine throughout the world. What would happen if our survival dictated that we fight again?

One evening the Director of the Institute for Advanced Study, J. Robert Oppenheimer, came to dinner at the graduate college and afterwards gave a talk. When it was over some of us hung around, sitting in a small circle at his feet. By midnight only four of us remained, yet he made no move to leave. His mood was melancholy, and I sensed he was lonely. Outside, the world seemed completely still. I took his lingering as a sign of willingness to speak more personally, so I asked him how he felt about bringing the atomic bomb into the world.

He spoke in hushed tones and with such a heavy heart that it was painful to be in his presence. He seemed like a character in a Greek tragedy, without distance or choice, caught up in a somber melodrama. He had just been through the humiliating ordeal of losing his security clearance, taken from him by the government he had served so ably as wartime leader of the Manhattan Project. No doubt this was part of the reason for his tone of weary resignation. But there was more. This man had played a central role in building the most destructive weapon ever used. Few faulted him for that. I certainly didn't. But there it was. The technical challenge, the glamour, the secrecy, the supreme urgency had carried him and others headlong, and the result had been agonizing death for more than 100,000 Japanese civilians and a world forever afterwards vulnerable to a nuclear holocaust.

I thought of my volcano and the glamour it had brought me, and how a taste for glamour had been part of what put me on the path to Princeton where I would hear Oppenheimer's cautionary tale. Questions about nuclear weapons were seeded that evening which, though they took decades to germinate, would eventually take me to the Soviet Union in search of a better game than war.

Guillotined at the Gate

A month into my first term at Princeton, I came down with mononucleosis. Most likely the all-nighters at Bell Labs, combined with weekend visits to Cape Cod to see Ruth, had lowered my resistance to this enervating student ailment. It couldn't have picked a worse time to send me home.

Once again at Princeton, as during my first semester at Oberlin, I had jumped in over my head. If I had any chance of making it back to the surface, missing the first few weeks of classes certainly shortened the odds. For some inexplicable reason, I didn't use the few hours of alertness that the disease afforded me to keep up with the work I was missing. Instead, I read a book called *A Biographical History of the French Revolution*[11] that brought back memories of *Les Misérables*, and nourished dreams of social justice that had been seeded at Oberlin.

When I returned to classes, I found myself hopelessly behind. There were no exams in graduate physics so my desperate situation was hidden from my professors. Evidently, it was not considered necessary to check up on our progress (or lack of it) apart from the one comprehensive exam that we all took at the end of our second year. Had there been course exams, the fact that I'd fallen behind would have been obvious to everyone, and my own fears corroborated. Instead, I scrambled to catch up over Christmas break, and hoped that new courses, beginning in the spring, would give me a second chance to take hold.

One-Upmanship

A few years earlier, a book called *One-Upmanship*[12] had given a name to the practice of putting others down by appearing to know more, have wider experience, and be better connected. As it turned out, that little book provided a more accurate model of the education I received than any college catalog. *One-Upmanship* was to academics what Machiavelli's *The Prince* was to statesmen.

Although knowledge was worshipped, the business of transmitting it was often shortchanged. For many students and some professors the primary satisfaction lay not in the learning and teaching but rather in ranking the abilities and contributions of others and demeaning presumed inferiors. This kind of behavior was modeled for students by world famous scientists. On one occasion I saw Nobel-laureate Wolfgang Pauli reduce a graduate student to tears. Part way into the student's presentation, Pauli announced that what we were being told was wrong and if anyone cared he would be glad to present a correct theory. As the assault continued, the young man broke down. Mercifully, Oppenheimer intervened to stop the savaging, and protectively led the graduate student from the room.

Derision and humiliation were common. Daily tea was rife with barbs and insinuations. If you asked a question, you had to be prepared for a condescending putdown like, "Oh, that's trivial," and then a breezy snow job, the goal of which was to show you your place. Knowledge is indeed power and some, afraid of losing their precarious edge, are loathe to share it.

Judd Fermi and I rented a small house in Princeton and often went to tea together. We found the hauteur of one aspiring mathematician to be particularly annoying and, behind his back, we called him the "Evil Genius." Later, when I met this fellow's dissertation advisor, I realized that he was merely imitating his professor's arrogance. It was hard to avoid being drawn into this vicious game. In a culture of predators and prey, the impulse to affirm one's superiority by putting down someone weaker is almost irresistible. As a frequent target, I was only dimly aware that my tormentors were themselves victims of put downs from more advanced students.

Creative elites of all sorts—not just mathematicians and physicists—cultivate an air of superiority and mystery, and often resist sharing their knowledge and wisdom. I remember my surprise when I read in the preface to a well-known mathematics text the author's promise to give away the trade secrets in his field, and my growing amazement and gratitude as I discovered he was actually keeping his word.[13] Much science and mathematics teaching is needlessly obscure, with obfuscation serving the purpose of limiting membership in the guild. Similarly, quite a few spiritual teachers trade in mystification to postpone the day when their students will threaten their authority, status, and income.

I had begun questioning the conventional understanding of genius even before I arrived at Princeton. Growing up in the shadow of Bell Labs, I'd gotten a behind-the-scenes look at several famous scientists who worked there. When my parents entertained my father's colleagues, I would spy on them, always trying to figure out if there was something about them that made them fundamentally different from me, or if in fact people were more alike than the disparities in their reputations suggested.

Getting an up close and personal look at the lives and work of people the public took for geniuses caused me to question the conventional wisdom—that these people were a distinct breed.

It would be decades before I found an explanation for scientific breakthroughs that didn't rest on the circular argument that the discoverers were simply geniuses. Later, I would see my question about genius as a special case of what I thought of as my Martian question, which, despite its tongue-in-cheek phrasing, would again and again give direction to my life: Are there Martians?

At various times, I would wonder if the French, the Germans, the Russians, the Chinese, or various fundamentalist sects were Martians, that is, were our differences irreconcilable?

Both my Martian and genius questions are questions of belonging. Despite our apparent differences, do we all belong to the same "tribe"? Is belonging inherently exclusive, or could it someday be all-inclusive? Would there always be Arlenes in the hall, or would we eventually let them in?

Nobody Unmasked: I Become Arlene

At Princeton, the experience I'd narrowly escaped at Oberlin was to be mine: this time I was in too far over my head and couldn't make it back to the surface.

No one except me knew how ill prepared I was to stand for the General Exam—the week-long written and oral test that was the gateway to doctoral research. As the day of reckoning approached, I sensed that I needed a year to grow up and catch up, and I wanted to do this as far away from Princeton as possible. The physics departments at Princeton and the École Normale Supérieure in Paris often exchanged a few students. Before revealing my ignorance on the exam, I had applied for a French Government Scholarship and arranged to spend the year following at the École Normale Supérieure.

When the exam results were announced, I was told that I'd have to retake the test. And like Arlene, who moved away shortly after her humiliation, I disappeared.[14]

6 | American in Paris

(1957–1958)

What one knows is, in youth, of little moment; they know enough who know how to learn.

– Henry Adams, *The Education of Henry Adams*[15]

The Battlefield

I sailed to France on the Queen Elizabeth in the fall of 1957, just months before Boeing's new 707 jets put ocean liners out of business. As the great ship approached Normandy my head was full of the war that a dozen years prior had raged in these very waters—the war I'd spent my earliest years playacting in my sandbox. A shipmate's brother had been killed in the D-day landings, and as we approached the coast he broke into tears.

On the train ride to Paris I peered out the window searching for signs of destruction. Nothing. After a few weeks of settling in, I persuaded the other Princeton exchange student, David Larson, to make a quick trip to Munich before fall term began. We rented a Lambretta motor scooter and took off for Germany. My quest was for signs of war in the land of the losers. The only evidence I found was a mountain of rubble on the outskirts of Munich. That mountain was the old city, and to my disappointment a new one had already risen in its place.

Horror

But not far from Munich we found the ruins of the concentration camp at Dachau. I thought of the Jews in my hometown, immigrants from turn-of-the-century pogroms in Russia. Jews were not singled out for special attention in Chatham; anti-Semitism struck no chord with us.

One of my friends, Maurice Best, was the slugger on our baseball team and seemed to hold the position of class president for life. His bearded father dressed in a black robe and looked the stereotype of the Old World Jew. I remember once looking over his shoulder at the town swimming hole where he was reading a fat tome. He showed me his book and I was startled to discover that not only were the words unrecognizable, the alphabet in which they were written was unfamiliar as well. He explained that the book was in Russian, by a famous author, Leo Tolstoy, and it was called *War and Peace*. I decided that some day I would read it.

On the way back to Paris, going too fast in a rainstorm, my co-explorer Dave drove our Lambretta off the road. My year abroad might have ended there, but, after soaring through the air, we landed shaken up but intact in an open field. When we got home and settled into our rooms at the École, Dave bought himself a Vespa scooter. I preferred walking and riding on the open platforms at the rear of Parisian buses. During our year together in Paris, Dave would be my mentor and my salvation.

École Normale Supérieure[16]

Until I was twenty I had never encountered a group of people who seemed that different from me. What I mean is that until then reason alone had been enough to account for, and usually settle, disagreements among us. Sure, there had been Dick Hughes in high school, an avid supporter of Senator Joe McCarthy, but Dick had just moved to town from Wisconsin, McCarthy's home state, and I attributed his obtuseness to chauvinism. Notwithstanding cases like Dick's, I assumed that people were essentially alike, and that what differences there were could be resolved with a combination of forbearance and bridge-building.

I returned from my quest for signs of war in Germany to discover that Paris was in turmoil over French policy in Algeria. Before the year was out I would witness demonstrations involving millions, the collapse of the Fourth Republic, and the return to power of the French wartime leader, General Charles de Gaulle.

At one point during the crisis there was a referendum on de Gaulle at the École. To my astonishment, de Gaulle got the

[52]

vote of just one of the three hundred Frenchmen. And that solitary vote came from a royalist who thought a de Gaulle presidency the closest thing to restoration of the monarchy. It puzzled me that the students, even though they were unanimously and vehemently opposed to French policy in Algeria, were even more hostile to de Gaulle who offered the best hope for avoiding civil war.

For the most part, French food was great. But they ate the mold on the cheese and they didn't have peanut butter. By Christmastime, I had developed a powerful longing for this American staple, and had asked for it at every grocery store in the Latin Quarter. French grocers would turn up their noses and scoff, "Only pigs eat peanuts!" In reaction to such galling insinuations the first of many Martian questions took shape in my mind—Are the French fundamentally different from Americans? Are they Martians?

French disdain for peanut butter was just a symbol of deeper differences. There were lots of things I couldn't agree on with my French friends, no matter how hard I tried. Yet most of the time I could see that they were just like Americans. This flip-flop of perspectives was common among the small contingent of foreign students—*pensionnaires étrangers*—which included two Americans (David Larson and myself), two Englishmen, and a solitary Irishman, German, Russian, Hungarian, Norwegian, Tunisian, Dane, Australian, and Swiss.

We foreigners often discussed the otherworldly traits of the French but, in our secret hearts, we suspected each other of being Martians as well. For example, the Irishman dismissed me as a heathen, and I regarded his religiosity as evidence of a medieval mindset. The Russian saw Westerners as capitalists living off the labor of the working class. The French *normalien*, as students at ENS are called, seemed to view all the foreign students as barbarians.

The epithets we had for each other—Frogs, Krauts, Limeys, Yanks, etc.—gave expression to the seemingly unbridgeable cultural and ideological differences that separated us. As I learned more about the Third Reich, Gallic exceptionalism paled beside Teutonic hubris. And for decades I would puzzle about the Russians. None of my "Martian questions" ever assumed more urgency than that one. As the nuclear arms race accelerated, my sophomoric question seemed tantamount to "war or peace?" War, if the Soviets insisted on forcing their political ideology on the world, and peace, if we could find a way to reconcile or sidestep our incompatibilities.

Apprenticeship with a Problem-Solver

It was in Paris that I finally hit upon a way of learning that worked. My countryman, Dave Larson, had aced the very general exam that I would have to retake at the end of that academic year. He was as skilled at one-upmanship as he was at physics, and his air of superiority infuriated the other students, who, as the cream of the French educational system, bowed to no one.

Though I recoiled at their condescension, I was in fact delighted when some of the French students, who hated Dave's arrogance as much I did, suspended his motor-scooter from one of the Sorbonne's spires. Stung by the prank, he cut off all contact with them and before long I was his only friend. Knowing that I had to retake the general exam, he offered to coach me by working our way through the problems in the text *Classical Electricity and Magnetism*.[17]

Every afternoon for months, I sat by his side as he tackled the problems. By the time we neared the end of the book, I had absorbed his methods.

I was traveling in Austria during summer vacation when word reached me that Dave had been killed by a Paris bus while riding his Vespa. All I could do was write his parents and tell them what Dave had done for me in the last year of his life.

Over the months that followed, I realized that I had learned enough from Dave to carry on without him.

§§§

Though I found the first ten minutes of many lectures inspiring, fifty minutes later I was often confused and frustrated. If only the professor would stop spewing out information until I'd mastered what he'd just said. If only his teaching was responsive to my questions—as it had been in my tutorials with Dave Larson. If only the pace were my pace— that of the learner—not that of the teacher. I wanted to verify each step before moving on to the next. Once the logical thread had been broken, I lost my grip on the argument.

Over the course of my formal education, I identified three ways that I could learn. I could work things out on my own; I could learn through apprenticeship; and I could learn by teaching others, as I had in high school.

Though I *attended* various schools, I was *educated* through apprenticeships. I never really liked schooling—the paternalism; the subordination to *others'* interests and pacing; the pressure, stress, and deadlines; the emphasis on *coverage* instead of *mastery*. It was because I passed rapidly through the schools I attended that I left as an apparent success—just months before I'd have been kicked out as a sorry failure. The difference between success and failure was narrow. I might never have noticed had my escapes not been so numerous.

Book of Books

In addition to my daily physics session with Larson, life in Paris was filled with Russian lessons at the Alliance Françoise (a stratagem for meeting girls); courting Suzanne, a German *au pair* from Hamburg; savoring French cuisine in the refectory at the École; exploring Paris (even the sewers of *Les Misérables*); and reading in my room.

Outside of science, I had never read much—until Paris. Supplied by the lending library at the American Cultural Center, just a short hop away on Bus # 27, I began reading voraciously. Fortunately, I began jotting down the titles and authors of books in a bound journal. And since I'd not been much of a reader prior to my sojourn in Paris, I added the titles of all the books I could recall reading up to that point. In the decades since, I've kept up the practice. If my house caught fire, the first thing I'd grab would be my "Book of Books." It comes closer to containing my life story than a photograph album ever could.

Over the Christmas break—my first away from home—I traveled to London where I stayed with Oberlin classmates, Richard and Carol Cooper. Dick was a Marshall Scholar in economics, and under his influence I began to devour books on economics, in particular Heilbruner's *Worldly Philosophers*, and the most widely used text of the day, Samuelson's *Economics*. My background in math made the going easier than expected. Witnessing the politics roiling France that year and seeing how Cooper's knowledge of the social sciences gave him a tool with which to analyze political and social change, I decided to devote myself to acquiring the economic tools to better understand politics.

At the end of spring term, in the company of my kindergarten friend Tom Purvis, I traveled through Western Europe on a Eurail pass, ending up at the Brussels World Fair, which was billed as a face-off between Western democracy and Soviet communism. The Soviets wanted to convince the world that their system was not only more productive, but more just. I wasn't persuaded by their propaganda, but the Fair left me with a strong desire to go see for myself.

A Stain Removed

Days later, I returned to New York on the ocean liner *S. S. United States*—reading *Moby-Dick* en route—just in time to retake the general exam in physics at Princeton and I passed. Not only had I learned enough from Dave Larson to apply his methods in other fields of physics, I think my brain had finally matured to the point where it was capable of grasping quantum theory. My mother volunteered the fifteen dollars required to convert passing the General Exam to a Master's degree. In the absence of either a high school or college degree, she was determined that I wouldn't leave Princeton without a diploma.

7 | Casting a Wider Net
(1958–59)

Branching Out

I had returned to Princeton and retaken the physics exam not to belong but to redeem myself. Pass or fail, I had decided I didn't belong in physics. A whole new world had seized my attention while in Europe—messy human problems of politics and justice in contrast to the tidy, objective problems of natural science—and before taking the physics exam, I'd arranged to study economics at the University of Chicago. As someone trained in math and physics, it was perhaps natural that I'd gravitate to the most quantitative of the social sciences.

It was not that my interests had suddenly shifted from science to human affairs. The personal problems of classmates had always interested me more than how things work. But for a long time I didn't realize that I might legitimately, and even productively, devote myself to anything other than physical science.

France had been in turmoil for most of my year there (1957–58). Millions marched in the streets carrying banners and chanting political slogans. I was an outsider, an onlooker. I did not fully understand the issues, but I did understand the *normaliens'* passionate opposition to colonialism, injustice, and inequity.

I had never seen anything like this in America. Moreover, my parents regarded demonstrative behavior of any kind as in poor taste. But the strong emotions the French showed for politics validated feelings I'd always had. What happened in Paris in 1957–1958 was a continuation of what I'd read about, and sympathized with, in Whitham's *Biographical History of the French Revolution*. Student protests echoed themes of social justice that had stirred my soul while reading Victor Hugo's *Les Misérables*.

In 1958, America wasn't ready to take on issues of social justice, in the streets or anywhere else, though a time of reckoning was much closer than most suspected.

Tasting Everything, Swallowing Nothing

I drove my 1950 Chevy from New Jersey to Chicago, rented a tiny basement apartment within walking distance of the University, and sold the car to a junkyard to make the first month's rent. I would earn enough to cover room and board as a research assistant doing calculations for one of the economics professors.

Everyone took the standard courses on price theory, macroeconomics, and money and banking (in which Milton Friedman lectured on the monetary theory that would subsequently make him an advisor to presidents and a Nobel laureate). Though my mathematical background gave me a leg up in quantitative courses like these, I found myself less interested in them than in the labor movement and anti-trust legislation. In the labor movement I saw how organizing many lesser forces could create a single force powerful enough to prevail against bullies like Burt and corporations like General Motors. From the start, the parts of economics that drew me were not its mathematical principles but rather the ways that people had found to shield themselves from abuses made possible by disparities in income and wealth.

I spent most of my time reading in my basement apartment. I hungrily consumed Thomas Wolfe's voracious quest novels—*Of Time and the River* and *The Web and the Rock*—and learned about the other side of his real-life love affair with Aline Bernstein in her account, *The Journey Down*. Wolfe's hero consumed not books, but libraries. His hunger resonated with me.

I also read W. Somerset Maugham's *Of Human Bondage* and *The Razor's Edge*. Maugham's *Writer's Notebook* in combination with Wolfe's *The Story of a Novel* and E. M. Forster's *Aspects of the Novel*. These books made me dream of writing, but it would be twenty-five years before I'd take that dream to heart.

Like many who read Jack Kerouac's bible for trans-continental pilgrims—*On the Road*—I spent several summers crisscrossing America in old cars fueled by 30 cent per gallon gasoline. Like a gerbil exploring its cage, I was driven to take in the whole thing while probing the limits of the Americentric vision I'd been raised on.

If *On the Road* fueled outward quests, the tale of interracial love that Kerouac told in *The Subterraneans* triggered an inward one. An African-American graduate student frequented one of the buildings in which I took economics classes, and though I admired her from afar, all I ever learned of her was her name—Easter.

The year in France had exposed me to socialist and communist doctrine. Many of the students at the École regarded themselves as one or the other, and were openly contemptuous of capitalism and American democracy. I was often tempted to point out that America had helped to deliver them from German occupation and get them back on their feet, but for the most part I held my tongue. On one occasion when France's humiliating defeat by the Germans did come up, the French countered by pointing out that it was the Soviet Red Army who defeated the Germans, not the Americans. Later, I would realize there was far more truth in this apportioning of credit than had been acknowledged in the West.

On the face of it, the brand of socialism advocated by the students at ENS sounded more compassionate and fairer than America's "winner take all" capitalism. But wasn't America richer than the socialist countries? What good is equality if it means everyone is equally poor?

I'd always been stirred by the egalitarian promises of Jeffersonian democracy, and America's failure to deliver on them had left me looking for something better. I turned to books outside the assigned economics texts, which, for the most part, extolled American capitalism. I read Max Eastman, Sidney Hook, Ludwig Feuerbach, Bertram Wolfe, Edmund Wilson, and Boris Pasternak's *Dr. Zhivago*. I also took a course by John U. Nef of Chicago's famously conservative Committee of Social Thought and was exposed to American conservatism before it surfaced in the administrations of Nixon, Ford, Reagan, and the Bushes.[18]

The net effect of French radicalism and Chicago conservatism was to make me want to go to Russia and see for myself how communism worked in practice. Coincidentally, President Eisenhower had just announced a student exchange program with the Soviet Union. In the naïve hope that the rudimentary Russian I'd picked up at Alliance Française would suffice, I applied. Those administering the program knew better and mercifully advised me to reapply when I knew more Russian. If I had gone to the USSR in 1959, I would have discovered ten years sooner than I did that claims of communist superiority were baseless.

During this period I conducted a sobering real-life experiment—with myself as subject. Ever since reading about famine in Pearl Buck's *The Good Earth*, I had wondered what it would feel like to starve. This may have had its roots, almost two decades prior, in the battle with my mother over whether I would eat her canned spinach. In any case, I resolved to find out how long I could go without food.

As it turned out, I lasted barely two days, during which I chronicled my condition. By the end, I was thinking of nothing but food. All my usual interests had evaporated within hours of skipping my first meal. At the movies, I noticed that the presence of anything edible on screen seized my attention to the exclusion of all else. As it grew, hunger accentuated my isolation and locked in my outsider status. I shunned all communication. I began hating anyone who was eating. How could they take food for granted, when I was so hungry? How could they be so callous and unconcerned? That they were unaware of my desperate cravings seemed no excuse.

Immediately upon breaking my fast—with a small glass of orange juice—I slept for four hours. Then I ate some bread and went back to sleep. It took several days for my body to return to normal.

Two years later, when Nigeria's ruling Ibo tribe used famine as a genocidal weapon of war against Biafran independence, I could not pry myself from the television. Images of African

children with bloated bellies and sticks for legs would recι
awful regularity into the twenty-first century.

Apprenticeship with a Model Builder

The most important learning of my life had begun quietly just
before my year in France and gained steam upon my return.
One of my fellow physics graduate students was a solitary
eccentric named Peter Putnam. He'd dropped out between
college and graduate school to study the work of the physicist
and philosopher Sir Arthur Eddington. Now, back at
Princeton, he pursued his personal vision with fierce
dedication. No one paid much attention to him.

When I asked him what he was doing, he replied, "Do you
really want to know?" Trapped, I said yes. His response
changed my life. He launched into a discourse on scientific and
moral law, arguing that causal and ethical principles could be
brought together by understanding how the mind works. He
saw the brain as a Darwinian machine that selected behaviors
according to whether or not the neural pathways that
represented them were self-reinforcing loops, all on a time scale
measured in fractions of a second rather than millennia. Our
conversation lasted all that day and continued in protracted
bursts for the next ten years.

Under the pretense of collaboration—he was actually a
mentor to me—we explored his model of brain function, and a
wide range of other topics, through hundreds of letters and
conversations. In addition, Putnam bombarded me with book-
length essays he was turning out on moral philosophy,
multiculturalism, the foundations of mathematics, and his
functional model of the nervous system. Though he wrote
constantly, he published little. Our working relationship
amounted to a comprehensive apprenticeship that was
fundamental to much of what I would do subsequently.

No one who knew Putnam doubted his genius. But the
way he expressed his ideas—referred to jokingly as
"Putnamese" by puzzled admirers—was too idiosyncratic to
penetrate the mainstream, and his work remains largely

unrecognized. To others has gone the credit for understanding the brain as a Darwin machine, though, as was the case with Gregor Mendel, proof of Putnam's precedence can be found in the few papers published during his lifetime.[19]

You're Nobody Till Somebody Loves You.[20]

When I did come out of my one-room basement apartment, it was usually to look for companionship. My friend Judd Fermi had grown up in Hyde Park. During our sophomore year at Oberlin, Judd's celebrated father, a pioneer in nuclear physics, had died of throat cancer—probably caused by exposure to radiation before its dangers were recognized. But his mother, Laura Fermi, still lived nearby, and she often invited me over for meals. She had written a bestseller called *Atoms in the Family*, as well as a biography of Mussolini, whose anti-Semitism had convinced her husband Enrico to take his Jewish wife and their two children directly to America from the Nobel ceremony in Stockholm. I wondered if you had to be as brilliant as Enrico to merit a woman as beautiful as Laura. Like her husband, she was ahead of her time. An admirer of Rachel Carson, she became one of the first environmental activists in her adopted country.

At one of her dinner parties I spotted a girl whom I'd seen around campus. I had been taken with the way she walked—a purposeful stride, devoid of vanity. Though she had drawn my eye, I was too shy to approach her directly. But Mrs. Fermi's introduction gave me the opening I needed.

Ann Lackritz was a Bryn Mawr graduate, now pursuing a Master's degree in Russian history at the University of Chicago. As we conversed, it struck me that this girl did not have a disingenuous molecule in her. That's what it was that had intrigued me about her carriage. The way people walk says a lot about them.

By the time we parted that evening, I had suggested another meeting. Within weeks, she was sharing meager meals of canned tuna and frozen lima beans in my cave. I regaled her with stories of Europe, which she had not seen even though she knew its history far better than I. We often pored over a map of Europe that I'd tacked to my wall and one day, on an impulse, I folded it into a large manila envelope and mailed it to her. When I saw her clasping the map as she hurried up to me in the alley behind my apartment, I knew she returned my feelings. Within the month we were living together. Ann had grown up in Chicago where her father was a successful jeweler with stores in Chicago and Beverly Hills. His luxurious home on the upper North Side was full of original works of modern art. He played the cello and held chamber music concerts in his living room, the centerpiece of which was a Steinway on which Vladimir Horowitz had performed for private parties.

Ann played the flute, and one of her teachers, William Kinkaid of the Philadelphia Orchestra, encouraged her to turn professional. Through her, I gained entrée into the world of art and, in playing duets with Ann for flute and piano, my love for classical music was renewed.

It soon became obvious that Ann had a natural aptitude for science. As a girl, she had never received a word of encouragement toward math or science. Most women of that era majored in either literature or history. At first, it was only the way her ears perked up at my occasional asides regarding science, but within months I found in Ann an extremely apt and eager student of math and physics and my occasional explanations turned into an ongoing tutorial.

I think her obvious talent and willing interest in matters scientific helped to rekindle my own. Through Ann, I met Robert Harris[21] who was studying quantum physics at Chicago. He and I decided to do what Larson and I had done the year prior: work through a graduate physics text together, this time Landau and Lifshitz's *Classical Theory of Fields*.

By summer I'd had enough of economics. Compared to the elegant, accurate theories of physics, economics models seemed imprecise, unreliable, and as much ideological as scientific. Given my growing passion for social issues, these limitations might have been set aside if I hadn't felt pressure building to embark on a career. Having a woman in my life made me understand, unconsciously if not consciously, that someday I might need to support a family. In the fifties, not everyone assumed, as Ann and I did, that women would work and earn a living. None of the women in my parents' world worked outside the home.

I began exploring alternatives to Princeton, for which I still harbored a bitter distaste, but I did so by writing Professor John Wheeler, one of the luminaries at Princeton who I'd come to know during my two years there. To my astonishment, he urged me to return to Princeton and work with him. When I responded that I wasn't interested in the field of general relativity—his current focus—he suggested a tidy problem in an area that he himself had pioneered in the late 1930s with Niels Bohr—nuclear fission.

I couldn't imagine myself leaving Chicago without Ann. Although we lived together there, going off to Princeton seemed to call for a formalization of our relationship. We decided to get married. I was twenty-two. Ann, a half-year older, had turned twenty-three.

My parents took the news without objections, but Ann's parents were opposed to their daughter marrying a Gentile— a "goy" in their terminology. I rather enjoyed being the object of a racial epithet, and embraced its use myself, while studiously avoiding the derogatory epithets then commonly leveled at Jews.

To lure Ann away from me, her parents made her an offer they thought she could not refuse: a lavish trip to Europe. She declined. When I let her father know that I was going to marry his daughter with or without his approval, he pivoted and threw an extravagant wedding party.

We left Chicago that evening and drove as far as Oberlin, Ohio where we spent our wedding night. Before driving on to Princeton, I gave Ann a tour of the campus where, four years prior, I had been an undergraduate. Had we been told that eleven years on we'd return to preside over the College as president and first lady, we would have dismissed the idea as preposterous.

8 | A Starter Identity
(1959–61)

During my year at the University of Chicago, I had begun two relationships that would give my life direction—partnership with Ann Lackritz and apprenticeship with John Wheeler. While the first of these was in the natural order of things, the epistolary relationship that I established with Wheeler that year was highly improbable, given my promiscuous relationship to physics.

Apprenticeship: Transmission of Mind

Professor John Archibald Wheeler was a bright star in the firmament of physics. On the eve of World War II, he and Niels Bohr had made a prediction about uranium that would prove critical to harnessing nuclear energy.[22] In the years following Einstein's death, it was Wheeler who gave new life to general relativity. He led the way into the no-man's-land where quantum and gravitational physics meet and gave black holes a central role in astrophysics.

But I had only just grasped the principles of quantum physics, and rather than follow Wheeler into the uncharted realm of astrophysics, I wanted to apply quantum theory to a down-to-earth problem. Wheeler accepted this preference and proposed that I try to account theoretically for the known fact that when a uranium nucleus splits, in addition to the fission fragments, a few neutrons are released.

There had been a moment when the future hinged on exactly how many neutrons are produced when uranium fissions. If the number is large enough, nuclear chain reactions are possible; if not, the feasibility, and therefore the threat, of nuclear weapons is greatly reduced.

When experiments showed that enough neutrons were released to sustain a nuclear chain reaction, Einstein was persuaded by Enrico Fermi and Leo Szilard (who was the first to see the possibility of a chain reaction) to alert President

Roosevelt to the grave military implications. Thus was born the Manhattan Project, which in turn led to nuclear weapons and the postwar nuclear arms race.

The problem Wheeler was proposing to me would provide a quantum-mechanical model of the self-sustaining reactions upon which the wholesale release of nuclear energy depended. Within weeks, I was immersed in an apprenticeship beyond price. It was like learning to hunt by stalking game with an experienced guide. I would save up my questions for our weekly sessions and Wheeler would address them in ways that pushed me beyond my limits. Sometimes I could sense that my mind was forming new neural connections as he spoke. He had a flair for metaphors and analogies, which I've always suspected he developed in *his* apprenticeship with Niels Bohr.

Most of our efforts ended in failure, but that didn't faze Wheeler. Failure was the norm. Trial and error was simply and unavoidably that part of research that preceded success. Invariably something about the way one approach failed would suggest another avenue worth pursuing. With renewed hope, I'd go off to explore that. Early the next morning the phone would ring and Wheeler would ask how things had turned out. I'd sheepishly admit the computations were not yet complete and wonder if he'd worked all night during the first year of his marriage.

Although passing on technical skills is an invaluable part of what goes on between mentor and student, something beyond that may also occur. In making me privy to his failures and his responses to failure, Wheeler was not merely modeling the scientific method, he was also showing me that he simultaneously devoted a part of himself to watching his own process.

By letting his students witness his witnessing faculty, he showed them how to develop a perceptive and robust witness in themselves. Acquiring the capacity to watch yourself with detachment and so gather accurate data from which you can build a model of your own model-building process is what apprentices need if they are to attain mastery.

I'm not sure that Wheeler was deliberately modeling the witness function, but there's no doubt that he did so. Good mentors show students how to solve problems; great mentors go a step further. By taking their students with them "behind the scenes" and inviting them to watch their witness in action, they activate the latent witness in their students. Guided by a witness that continually fine-tunes our quests, we pursue them more strategically.

Wheeler was working on a wide range of problems with other graduate students and colleagues, and he was so busy that I'd see him wherever I could—walking between office and home, on a train to New York, in a car to the airport. For the spring semester of 1960, Ann and I followed him to the University of California at Berkeley, where he had a sabbatical appointment as a visiting professor. We drove a Volkswagen Beetle across America to California. Somewhere along the way, we conceived our first child.

In Berkeley my expenses were covered by working as Wheeler's research assistant. I often felt I should have paid for the privilege, but that was not how things worked. I spent half my time on my dissertation and the other half performing calculations on a problem in relativity theory that Wheeler hoped would prove or disprove the possibility of time travel. Most professors would not have added the name of a human calculator to a paper, but that was not Wheeler's way. Not only did he add my name, he put it first! Never did Wheeler deviate from the convention of alphabetical order, and rarely was his name—beginning as it did with a "W"—other than last on his many collaborative efforts.

During the spring of 1960, working high above the Berkeley campus in the Lawrence Lab, I used a Marchant hand-calculator to plot results that are still cited in support of the argument that we cannot go back in time, even if we travel through wormholes in multiply-connected space-time.[23]

Wheeler kept his footing, despite a crowded, chaotic schedule, by focusing intensely on observing and understanding nature. Looking out to the Pacific one evening at dusk, he noticed a layer of smog above San Francisco. He immediately began formulating an atmospheric inversion model that would account for this blight and reveal what would have to be done to remove it.

At first I'd been embarrassed by Wheeler's royal treatment. I didn't feel special and saw no reason he should treat me like a prince. But I soon realized that he treated everyone with equal courtesy, from secretaries to students to famous colleagues. He saw potential contributors everywhere, and respectfully invited others to join him in his quest, or, with equal enthusiasm, supported them in pursuing their own. Still, as the beneficiary of his generosity, I felt I was creating an infinite indebtedness, one I would never be able to repay. Later, I came to understand the cardinal rule of apprenticeship: beneficiaries rarely if ever repay their mentors directly. Rather, the debt they incur is discharged by re-transmitting to others the "secrets" their teachers have shown them—the pay-it-forward principle.

Not that there are real secrets, intentionally withheld. Graduate physics is not a secret society. On the contrary, the theories and techniques of physics are available to anyone willing to study the literature. The secrets I refer to lie at a deeper level, and have to do with habits and qualities of mind of which the practitioners themselves are often only dimly aware. Most trained physicists have a working knowledge of the basic theories and problem-solving techniques. What distinguishes one from another is something more subtle and elusive. It could be called their "turn of mind," and it finds expression in all aspects of their lives, not just in how they pursue physics.

What is most valuable in an apprenticeship is the absorption of a mentor's uncanny sense for looking down the right alleys, for posing answerable questions, and for sensing which problems will bear fruit and which are better held for later. These skills go beyond what's conveyed in textbooks, and are subtler than the problem-solving techniques I'd acquired working alongside Dave Larson and Bobbie Harris.

Decades after working with Wheeler what I remember is his boyish enthusiasm. Imagination and tenacity blended harmoniously in him, and he modeled his personal synthesis of these two very different capacities for all who came in contact with him.

Like many creative thinkers, Wheeler had a penchant for turning conventional wisdom on its head. He loved to quote Niels Bohr to the effect that the opposite of a deep truth is also a deep truth. I remember his willingness to try just about anything to solve a problem, learn from his failures, and then rebound and try again and again. And if the problem still did not yield, then put it on the shelf and take another look at it five, ten, even twenty years later. Never give up. In a life lasting ninety-six years, he never did.[24]

A lot of attention is paid to the flair and originality of creative people. Equally important to their ultimate success is sheer persistence. Most successful people acknowledge that a stubborn unwillingness to give up was the main reason they ultimately succeeded. But what few recognize is that the tenacity they are able to bring to their quest is itself sustained by a foretaste of the promise and integrity of the idea that's gestating within them.

Long before they're actually born, new ideas may exert a pressure toward their own discovery. It's not so much that people grit their teeth and will themselves onward in the face of others' indifference, as it is that the ideas they're pursuing stoke the fires that keep them going.

So, if you find yourself rising early or working late on a quest that chose you as much as you chose it, count yourself lucky. Honor the demon that has taken possession of you. The will to persevere in the absence of recognition is granted to few. An outsized capacity for work is a sign that we're onto something before we know it ourselves.

Nothing that mentors transmit to their apprentices is more motivating than the invitation to take themselves seriously. It feels as if King Arthur has seated you at the Round Table and your quest actually matters to him and the fellowship of knights. Forever afterwards, your life is endowed with a certain seriousness. You never shake the sense that you're responsible for delivering on the promise your mentor has seen in you.

John Archibald Wheeler's nose for good questions, his can-do optimism, his capacity for hard work—starting immediately, continuing indefinitely—his acknowledgement of others, his metaphorical turn of mind, and above all, his taking me seriously, are as vivid to me today as in the days I spent in his company.

Who Needs Betty Friedan?

Most of the women I knew at Oberlin in the early fifties were intent on having a career. One of the women's dormitories even threw a party to celebrate the English language edition of Simone de Beauvoir's *The Second Sex*. Its publication in France (1949) had marked the birth of a second wave of feminist consciousness that, by century's end, would transform women's rights and roles worldwide.

Ann had instinctively adopted nascent feminist values and planned to get a job in either teaching or social work upon finishing a Masters degree in history. Then I came along and although she got her history degree, she realized that she'd rather develop her natural talent for math and science.

But Princeton University was for men only. Though Princeton would join the stampede to coeducation in 1972, the idea of women attending classes in 1959 was not only contrary to university policy, it was deemed presumptuous.

But not to Ann. She sought out the few professors of math and physics who might be sympathetic to the idea of having a woman in their classes and persuaded them to let her audit. Professor Ames devised a formula that neatly solved the problem of a female accumulating credit for work at Princeton. He proposed to write a letter, upon her completion of his course, that would read, "If Ann L. Fuller had been officially registered in this course, her grade would have been X." This work-around, which Ann persuaded other professors to adopt, would enable her, without ever paying a cent of tuition, to complete the course requirements for an undergraduate physics major at Princeton. As far as we know, she was the first woman to do so.

Giving Birth

For most of my first year with Wheeler, I searched for a way to solve the thesis problem he had suggested to me that wouldn't involve tedious numerical calculations. Not only did such a brute force approach seem inelegant, I'd had my fill of performing calculations by hand as Wheeler's assistant—"math slave" was what I called myself—on the question of time travel through worm holes.

By spring Ann's pregnancy was obvious, and, as we headed back to Princeton that summer, I was worried. A breakthrough seemed unlikely. That would mean no Ph.D., no job, no money.

Yet the schedule the baby was on made no allowances for the intractability of the equations describing nuclear fission. It was Wheeler who brought me to my senses. At his urging, I gave up my resistance to solving the problem numerically. In the four years since my all-night vigils with the primitive computer at Bell Labs, computers had gained in reliability, and could, if properly programmed, solve the quantum equations in hours. If I was going to provide for my family, I'd have to put my aesthetic scruples aside and partner with these new machines.

An ace programmer at a nearby government laboratory agreed to give me a private tutorial. No piece of pedagogy ever figured more directly in my getting a degree than this one. Within days, I was wondering why I had ever resisted computers. Programming digital computers in the newly available scientific programming language—Fortran—was easy and it was fun.[25]

An hour's train-ride from Princeton, at New York University, there was a state-of-the-art IBM computer into which I fed the punch cards that, an hour or so later, would spit out the results.

Moral: For every day you spend avoiding something, try it for at least a few minutes to be sure your distaste is well-founded.

At first, the computer printout made no sense. Since no one ever gets a complex numerical program right the first time, a period of debugging is the lot of all novices. And not until every last bug is identified and removed do the answers meet simple tests that show they could possibly be right.

On my third trip to the NYU computer, the numbers I was getting began to make sense. Soon they fell into a pattern that we had anticipated and I knew the program was sound. It was the Eureka moment for which every researcher yearns. Before boarding the train for Princeton, I bought Ann a bouquet of flowers. All that now stood between me and my degree was to run this program for a few dozen cases of physical interest, plot the results, and write up and defend the thesis.

My gestation period had been about eighteen months—double Ann's. Our daughter Karen's first year in Princeton was our last. Neither pregnancy nor the birth itself had slowed Ann's progress through the undergraduate curriculum in physics.

For me, twenty years of schooling were coming to an end. Ever since high school, I'd been in a hurry. Perhaps I knew that if I went any slower, the powers that be might realize that I didn't know much, and kick me out.

Feigning Equality

The final requirement for the Ph.D. was an oral defense of the thesis before a handful of professors chosen for their knowledge of your field. One of the professors Wheeler asked to serve was Marvin "Murph" Goldberger, a disciple of Enrico Fermi, a future president of Cal Tech and Director of Princeton's Institute for Advanced Study. Graduate students held him in especially high regard, perhaps because he was that rare combination of smart and jolly.

Even though final oral exams were usually perfunctory, seldom exceeding an hour, Wheeler was taking no chances. He called me in for a dry run, and in parting suggested that I bone up on a paper that Goldberger had written ten years prior that bore a tangential relationship to my thesis.

By the day of my orals, I knew Goldberger's paper by heart. Sure enough, this was where Murph took the questioning. Without letting on that I had studied his paper, I derived his key result from first principles, proceeding with starts and fits so he wouldn't catch on, but fast enough to dazzle him. After the exam, there were handshakes all around and much conviviality. If Goldberger suspected my little deception, he kept it to himself.

After Wheeler's doctoral students defended their dissertations, he gave a party for them and their friends. This was actually the scariest moment in the entire two year process, for it was understood by all that this was when you stopped addressing your mentor as "Professor" and began to call him by his first name.

If you were going to succeed on your own, breaking certain ingrained deferential habits was a must. Using first names marked a profound psychological shift—a change that was essential to realizing your full potential. It felt a bit like calling Einstein "dude," but somehow I got "John" out of my mouth. Never was I comfortable calling him "Johnny," the name he was known by throughout the world of physics.

The anxiety over addressing my professor on a first name basis was my first conscious encounter with the power of transference, or in Ernest Becker's illuminating phrase, "the spell cast by persons."[26] Such spells entail a transfer of power. Transference exists between teachers and students, celebrities and their fans, gurus and devotees, spouses, parents and children, leaders and followers. It seems we can't mature without transference, but neither can we reach our full maturity without ridding ourselves of its disempowering effects.

Like an image gaining definition as it rises out of a cloudy Polaroid, a workable identity was coming into focus. For the first, but not the last time, I had an answer to the question:

Who am I? By teaming up with Ann and getting a doctorate, I had, at last, put together the rudiments of an identity.

A Marketable Identity

After Sputnik and before Baby Boomers flooded the market, physicists were scarce and jobs plentiful. Plus, it didn't hurt to be a Wheeler student. A note from him to colleagues at two universities was all it took to get me two job offers, a postdoc at the University of California at Berkeley and an Instructorship at Columbia University in New York City. I chose Columbia because I knew that the only way I would ever understand physics was to teach it.

The department chair, a big-hearted man named after a medieval saint—Polykarp Kusch—asked me to teach the graduate course in mathematical methods of physics. I was both thrilled and scared, but I wrote him saying I would give my left arm for the opportunity. Again, I felt that I should be paying Columbia University for the privilege, not the other way round.

We spent the summer of 1961 in Amherst, Massachusetts, where Ann and I and nine month-old Karen rented a house so I could work with Peter Putnam while I prepared to teach the course at Columbia on mathematical physics.

That summer, in between the last of my schooling and my first real job, I was in heaven. Although I had no high school diploma and no bachelor's degree, I did have a Ph.D. and that was all anyone cared about. I had a good job, and a wife whom I loved and admired.

My academic appointment had silenced my parents' doubts and, once again, they were proud of me. But, within months of settling into my office at Columbia, cracks in my identity appeared.

9 | A Case of Mistaken Identity
(1961–1967)

Genghis in Academia

Princeton and Columbia, though both in the forefront of physics, couldn't have been more different. Princeton had an old world flavor, the professors were gentlemen, and research into the big questions set the tone. Columbia was New York City-flavored, the professors competed openly with each other, and research focused on issues of immediate consequence to the development of physics and careers.

In the elevator at Columbia colleagues would ask "What results have you gotten this week?" One battle-scarred professor confided to me "It's not enough for you to succeed; your colleagues must fail." Years later I realized he was plagiarizing Genghis Khan, but even then I knew that competitiveness carried to that extreme was toxic.

At Princeton, the competition was no less intense, but it was more genteel. Strolling across the campus or sipping tea, colleagues would wax sublime about the mysteries of the universe. What Princeton and Columbia professors shared was an unflagging search for new truth that could be rigorously demonstrated to skeptical, exacting colleagues.

A parade of Nobel Laureates passed through the places I worked and studied—Bell Labs, Princeton, Berkeley, and Columbia——and I knew many of them. My department chair at Columbia, the aforementioned Polykarp Kusch, exhibited an uncommon modesty when he said, "There are two kinds of Nobel Prize winners: the kind that make the Prize famous, and the kind that are made famous by the Prize. I am of the latter variety."

From close inspection, I came to see that those the public saw as geniuses were not fundamentally different from my fellow graduate students. And I was a typical graduate student. Since I knew I was not fundamentally different from the kids in my grade school, it followed that these scientists, although lionized and honored, did not differ in their basic make-up and native capabilities from my classmates, half of whom had been written off as "dumb kids." If this hunch were true, it held the seeds of a far-reaching change in how we see ourselves and others.

Since second grade I'd puzzled over the difference between smart kids and dumb kids. By my mid-twenties, it seemed to me that the obvious differences between these famous professors and my grade school classmates could be accounted for without invoking the mystery of "genius," and that these differences were neither innate nor immutable. On the contrary, they could be greatly narrowed, if not eliminated, by providing children with apprenticeships—beginning in infancy—as good as the ones I'd had.

Instead of deciding in advance what students will learn and trying to cram it into them, teachers would have to tailor a curriculum geared to the varied interests and different cognitive styles of learners. What that meant to me was that, as the economies of the world grew rich enough to support individualized education, we'd be able to educate kids like those in my elementary school—including Arlene—to be creative adults.

It's not for lack of potential that the world is short of excellence. It's because opportunities for contact with good role models are limited and schooling is replete with indignities that persuade most people that they're not cut out for creative work. This is perhaps understandable so long as work consists of routine repetition for which the main qualification is a willingness to follow orders. But it's clearly unsuited to knowledge-based societies in which career changes are the rule, not the exception.

Every so often during my on-again, off-again romance with physics I'd found myself asking, "Is that all there is?" My passion for physics was inconstant. I was more in love with the mathematical beauty of physics models than with understanding how the physical world worked.

What I did want was to understand why I felt I belonged when I did, and why, more often, I felt like an outsider. The circles in which I moved rationed acceptance as if it were rice in a famine. In one of those life-changing revelations, I realized it had always been so. The beauty and glamour of physics had beguiled me, deflecting my attention from issues of inclusion and exclusion that had intrigued me since childhood. Those problems had never stopped whispering to me and now they were yelling. I knew they wouldn't let me go until I gave them their due.

Under financial and social pressure, I had managed to put together a makeshift identity as a physicist. There is nothing like necessity, especially that imposed by parenthood, to accelerate the formation of identity. Physics was the suit of clothes closest to hand when reality knocked and, mindless of the fit, I'd hastily put it on.

For a time the rarefied atmosphere at Columbia, and the fact that I was finally learning physics—by teaching it—kept me going. Departmental practice dictated that I teach the same course three years in a row, a system that capitalized on the investment it took to create the lectures the first year by reaping the reward of two easy repeat performances. If, during the first year, I was only a few months ahead of my students, in the second year I felt like an old hand.

Although my performance was more polished that second year, to my puzzlement, I enjoyed it less. I rated the first two years gold and silver, and began the third anticipating bronze. Two weeks into it, I realized that year three was mud. When I stopped learning, I lost heart for teaching.

During that third year, I offered a new course on Einstein's relativity theories and, as I prepared to teach this material, my enthusiasm for physics flared up again. But by the second pass through general relativity, even its unsurpassed beauty did not move me. Messy human issues kept grabbing my attention, leading me further and further from physics. I would lock the door to my office and bury myself in literary masterpieces and political theory. Resorting to my old formula of one chapter a day, I worked my way through George Sabine's *History of Political Thought*.[27] I spent a lot of time discussing radical theories of education with another dreamer, my departmental colleague Daniel Greenberg, who would soon leave Columbia to start the Sudbury Valley School in Massachusetts.[28]

The Origin of Order

For several years, I tried to find a niche for myself in the nascent field of neuroscience. For almost a decade, I had worked to understand Putnam's model of the nervous system well enough to explain it to others. Toward the end of my stay at Columbia, I enrolled in a class of medical students and dissected a human brain. As my five years at Columbia came to a close, I began giving colloquia on Putnam's Darwinian model of brain function at universities around the country,[29] sometimes in the context of auditioning for a job.

Putnam had also done a conventional physics thesis with Wheeler, and we kept our mentor informed about our work on brain function. As it progressed, he arranged for us to give a seminar at Princeton to a group of his graduate students and colleagues. I led off—the idea being that my exposition was likely to be more understandable than Putnam's (the world's sole speaker of the now-extinct language of *Putnamese*). Putnam would weigh in during the question period. From these attempts at exposition, I worked up a publishable version of Putnam's theory which we titled *On the Origin of Order in Behavior*. Renegade physicist David Bohm championed the model and secured its publication in a professional journal.[30]

Looking back on my decade-long attempt to make Putnam's thought comprehensible and more widely known, I'm struck by the irony that, given my penchant for demystification, I was myself drawn to a philosopher whose writings were inaccessible and idiosyncratic. Peter Putnam was killed by a bus in a traffic accident, like my fellow student and teacher Dave Larson. A highly original and comprehensive thinker, Putnam has yet to receive the recognition his work deserves. A biographical note and some of his papers are available on the Web.[31]

In the Columbia physics department, intellectual interests that strayed beyond physics were regarded with skepticism if not disdain. Walking the corridors, teaching my classes, and at afternoon tea, I began to feel like a fake. My professorial status was a cover story shielding my true identity from colleagues and students—and obscuring it even to myself. I began to think my days as a physics professor were numbered, yet I didn't see a way to make a living without keeping up the charade. Even though research-oriented Columbia didn't want me, I probably could have made a living teaching physics somewhere.

"Did You Ask a Good Question Today?"

There was one professor at Columbia with whom I accidentally slipped into a mentor-apprentice relationship. Israel Isidor ("Izzy") Rabi was Columbia's most famous physicist. He had been the first recipient of the Nobel Prize after World War II. In giving the honor to Rabi, an American Jew, the committee was also condemning Germany's racist politics and signaling its recognition that, during the war, the center of world physics had shifted from Europe to America.

Rabi's wartime work had been in the development of radar, and afterwards he argued that although the Bomb had ended the war, it was radar that won it. He was one of the first and most effective of the new breed of citizen-scientists that included Enrico Fermi and J. Robert Oppenheimer. He also served as mentor to many young physicists who went on to make seminal contributions to science.

Rabi had been born at the end of the nineteenth century in what is now Poland. By the time I got to Columbia he was a scientific elder statesman. As the dean of American physics, he spent as much time in Washington as he did on campus. Still, Columbia expected him to teach at least one course. At the start of my third year at Columbia, claiming he'd been summoned by President Kennedy, Rabi phoned me at home one evening to ask if I could substitute for him the next morning. I spent the night frantically boning up on the kinetic theory of gases.

Upon his return, Rabi asked how it had gone and when I said I had enjoyed it, he suggested that I take over the rest of the course. He wasn't too proud to admit that, along with the Washington trips, he was finding it increasingly difficult to teach modern statistical mechanics.

I gave myself a crash course in the subject and for the next several years, made Rabi's course my own. Along with the chance to learn something about this corner of physics came an unadvertised bonus that was beyond expectation and worth any price: I got to hang out with Rabi for hours at a stretch.

We never talked physics. Instead he regaled me with anecdotes of his life and times, peppering them with his insights into people and their motives. Rabi was an imp and he delighted in gossiping about everyone he knew—and he knew everyone.

More important than the stories themselves, which were immensely entertaining, was the enlightened perspective he brought to human affairs. For a precious few years, Rabi was an official advisor to the president and a secret guru to me. What made him special was an elfin quality and his unguarded talk. I remember running into him years later and, skipping the usual pleasantries, he grinned and announced, "Today I am three score and ten and ten percent." I did the math and realized that he was announcing his seventy-seventh birthday. He was always a boy at heart—playful, inquisitive, and light-hearted, even about the most serious matters. Experiencing Rabi's curiosity and passion for topics other than physics encouraged me to take my own questions—which were then leading me away from it—seriously.

Toward the end of his days, he was quoted in the New York Times as saying, "Every other Jewish mother in Brooklyn would ask her child after school: 'So? Did you learn anything today?' But not my mother. 'Izzy,' she would say, 'did you ask a good question today?'"

I remember Rabi as a mischievous mentor, Groucho Marx to Wheeler's Ralph Waldo Emerson.

The Chalk Drops

As I began my fifth year at Columbia, I knew I had to get out. A lack of results in pure physics meant that there was no chance of a permanent position. Columbia had even denied tenure to Steven Weinberg, one of my Princeton classmates who would go on to win the Nobel for his theory of the weak interaction (one of Nature's four known forces). When I'd accepted the offer from Columbia, Chairman Polykarp Kusch had told me bluntly, "If you win the Nobel prize before you come up for reappointment, we'll consider you for tenure. Otherwise, forget it." I had appreciated his straight talk then, and I thought it wise to take action before I was officially booted out.

Quite apart from the judgment of others, there was something growing within me that could no longer be stifled. Five years into my physics career at Columbia, and about half-way through the mud phase of the course on statistical mechanics, I was writing equations on the blackboard when the chalk fell out of my hand and landed in the tray below. It lay there while I stood, surprised and embarrassed, trying to gather the will to lift it and continue scribbling on the blackboard. With an enormous effort I finally did, but the minute the class was over I went home and said to Ann, "The chalk has dropped." It did not feel as if I had intentionally let go of it, but rather that the chalk suddenly weighed a ton and an irresistible force had pulled it from my hand.

Finishing School

Once again, Wheeler came to the rescue. He arranged for both Putnam and me to spend a year at Wesleyan University's Center for Advanced Study, a place you could do anything you wanted—but only for one year. Putnam declined the offer, preferring to remain in New York City for reasons of his own.

The one- year limit made me feel a little like Cinderella at the ball but at least I had put off the day of reckoning.

Wesleyan University had been the beneficiary of a large bequest of Xerox stock and by the late sixties had money to burn. It used it to establish a think-tank for a few academics and public intellectuals. As a gesture to the sciences, a scientist was included in the mix, and for the academic year 1967–68, I became their token geek.

As a fellow at Wesleyan's Center, I would spend a year in the company of the poet Stephen Spender; the literary critic Ivor A. Richards; the classicist William Arrowsmith; and Richard Goodwin, one-time political advisor to Presidents Kennedy and Johnson—all under the urbane directorship of Paul Horgan, who had himself won a Pulitzer Prize for his history of the Rio Grande.[32]

Wesleyan served me as a kind of finishing school. I spent most of my time in conversation with these literary lions. Richards's observation that "we are all products of the assistance we are able to accept" put into words something I'd always felt but never acknowledged.

While at Wesleyan, I offered a course on Peter Putnam's philosophy, and at Horgan's request, presented a so-called Monday Evening Paper based on Putnam's ideas entitled *Causal and Moral Law*. In science, hypotheses are tested in laboratory experiments. Knowing nature's laws enable us to harness her power. Moral laws, on the other hand, are intuitive insights of great generality which appear to come from nowhere and gain their credibility through tradition. I argued that moral law also had its origins in observation and evidence which were then summarized in the form of maxims, precepts, rules of thumb, and commandments. With the talk at Wesleyan's Center, I completed my apprenticeship with Putnam, for it was his philosophy of morals that had drawn me to him ten years prior.

§§§

When the year at Wesleyan ended, I took a position at the Battelle Institute in Seattle, a scientific research firm with branch laboratories around the world. My goal was to put the finishing touches on a book I was co-authoring with Fred W. Byron, Jr. that was based on the mathematical physics course I'd developed at Columbia. I was determined to put everything I knew about mathematics and physics into it because I knew it was my swan song. Though it was officially titled *Mathematics of Classical and Quantum Physics*, I always thought of it as "Farewell to Physics," echoing the title of a book by Paul Gallico—*Farewell to Sport*—that he wrote as he left sports-writing for fiction.[33]

For ten years I had struggled to remain faithful to physics. Although I loved its elegant models, I knew it would never fully engage both my mind and heart. As the romance wore thin, I'd tried to maintain a link to my formal training by styling my work on Putnam's brain models as biophysics. However, my daydreams and preoccupations left no doubt that this too was just another cover story. When I finished the textbook on mathematical physics, I left physics, never to return, but never to forget. Forty years on, my pulse still quickens when I read of a breakthrough in mathematics, physics, or cosmology.

Cover Stories

Cover stories are often required to keep the wolves at bay. But unless we realize that a tired old identity has turned into an act, it can imprison us. Many jobs serve their holders as cover stories from day one. Chance, aptitude, status-seeking, and expectations of family, friends, and self may inveigle us into taking roads more traveled that disregard our inclinations. The need to belong can blind us to the compromises we make to get into the club.

Rare is the job that never requires you to pretend it's your life. But when you realize you're faking enthusiasm, you may be able to shift direction within the job or modify it so it aligns more closely with your passion. And, as was the case with my physics, it may prove to have been useful, even essential, preparation for one's life's work.

My brief career in physics taught me how to think abstractly—for example, to require of models that they possess symmetry and invariance—and it also provided me with a credential that persuaded others to give me a chance in areas where I lacked experience.

The defiance of "take this job and shove it" is something few can afford. Putting self-realization ahead of family obligations is selfish, and those who do so are usually condemned. But, if the gamble pays off, then all is forgiven and what was at first seen as irresponsibility is reinterpreted as integrity and courage.

The main thing is not to fool *oneself*. It's no crime to let others believe we are our title, but it's a disservice to ourselves. Speaking in disguise to his men, who believed him to be one of them, Shakespeare's King Henry said, "I think the king is but a man, as I am: the violet smells to him as it doth to me." No wonder he was an inspirational leader.

Admitting to ourselves that we're under cover on the job is the first step in forming a new identity. Many who escape the closet of a cover story testify to the fact that it's possible to prepare a new identity while working a forty-hour week incognito in the old one. If the only way to change one's feathers were to go cold turkey, far fewer would opt to put themselves and their dependents at risk.

No matter how developed a new identity may be— incubating within the chrysalis of the old one—exiting the cocoon is hazardous. Leaving a job and leaving a relationship have something in common. Often, there's no going back, and no security going forward. Both transitions can produce sharp discontinuities in identity. If you have mouths to feed, no one will hold it against you if you spurn your dream. But since an example is set for others whatever we do, it's never an easy choice.

Often there's a way both to provide for everyone affected and at the same time to follow your heart, whether it's to a new partner or new work. A mathematics teacher of mine, who, in his sixties, ended an unhappy marriage of three decades, brightened when he realized that statistically two of his four kids would experience divorce, so divorced or not he'd be serving as a role model for half his children.

It's not so much *what* we do as *how* we do it. By admitting mistakes, showing care for all involved, and taking responsibility, even those who criticize you for following your passion are apt, in their own secret hearts, to envy you.

America's Story Shapes My Own

Every man's life is in itself a story, where there are heroes and monsters and perils to overcome. There is lust and defeat and humiliation. A man finds his life in the story he tells of it. ... It's the same for a people, for a country. A people make up a large tale in which every separate man may place his own smaller tale. And soon the story and the people are one and the same.

– G. F. Michelsen

At five, with my nation unwilling to take a stand in the looming global conflict, I refused to take boxing lessons at the YMCA. As America discovered her strength in World War II, I too was emboldened. Teenage derring-do echoed America's boldness on the world stage—helping rebuild postwar Europe, assembling a nuclear arsenal, taking a stand in Korea. Teenage doubts were mirrored in the confused national paranoia of the McCarthy era. In the manner of young adults, I patronized my parents on domestic politics as America lectured the Old World. As I married, had a child, and took my first job, America was harking to the call of a vigorous, young John F. Kennedy. Teaching physics at Columbia while my country roused itself from the somnolent fifties, I felt, for a brief shining moment, that I too had a place in Camelot.

It was not to last, for me or my country. Kennedy, in addition to proposing a trip to the moon, sent "advisors" to Vietnam. Both initiatives would reverberate long beyond his thousand days. But what was most important about Kennedy's leadership was that he posed questions that Americans were at last ready to hear: Were we living up to our ideals? Were we doing our best?

The right questions, asked at the right time, can stir a nation's conscience and inspire a people. Deep down, we all knew the answer to both of the president's questions was "No." Kennedy's charm and optimism stirred many to heed his call. His timely challenge helped make the sixties the transformational years they were. We either had to admit that "All men are created equal" was merely window-dressing, or change our country and ourselves.

That was the battle I wanted to be part of. Like my personal quest, it was about who belongs and who does not.

10 | Steps toward a New Identity
(1967–1968)

"Why Isn't Everyone Black?"

By 1967, inner cities all across America were in turmoil. Not far from where I was working in Seattle, local television was reporting mounting rage in Seattle's ghetto. The dropout rate at Garfield High School was off the chart.

I was at the Battelle think tank preparing my math book for publication when an idea grabbed me and wouldn't let go. I drove my Beetle to the high school and asked the principal to let me offer a course that I believed would reduce the dropout rate.

When he explained that he couldn't take kids out of regular classes to serve as my guinea pigs, I proposed to begin with kids who'd already dropped out and were hanging around and getting into trouble. The principal figured these kids were beyond both harm and salvation, and that a class with me might keep them out of his hair.

The kids they gave me reminded me of myself—once they lost the scent of learning, they stopped paying attention and became restless. And most of them had lost the scent years earlier. I wanted to prove that, *if they were interested,* they could learn. They'd already been written off as the dumbest of the dumb, so if they could learn, *anyone* could.

The key, I discovered, was that before they would listen to me, I had to listen to them. They had been ignored and mistreated all their lives, and they would not even look at me until I showed them that their opinions mattered.

I did this by teaching them *only what they said they wanted to know.* I told my group of twenty boys that their concerns would set the agenda and that I intended to stop the moment I detected boredom and move on to whatever anyone suggested.

Since they had different interests, this meant shifting topics when even a single boy lost interest.

When I didn't know enough about something to teach it, I'd say so, and study up so that if it ever came up again I'd be ready. I found that when the students were asking about things they wanted to know, they kept asking the same questions until they were satisfied. The characteristic rhythm of this class was jumpy, constantly moving from topic to topic.

The course began, not surprisingly, with a sex-related question tossed out by one of the students. It continued as the rest of the class hollered questions—on sex, drugs, race, justice, and death. Chasing their questions reminded me of chasing a soccer ball as it caromed around the playing field.

The day the first heart transplant was announced they were placing bets among themselves on the patient's survival. Most believed he would live—initial reports had been optimistic. I surprised them by betting that he wouldn't. "Why throw your money away?" they asked—a genuine question, eliciting a brief explanation of how the body can recognize foreign substances—like germs and transplanted organs—and attack them, killing the recipients of the new organs.

"But kidney transplants work okay. Why don't those people all die?" An opportunity to explain how the body's natural defenses can sometimes be tricked by drugs and radiation treatment.

"I thought radiation could sterilize you!" one kid hollers. "Is sterilization like using rubbers?" someone asks. Class interest soars. A discussion of contraception follows. Then, "Does smoking grass keep you from having babies?"

With this question, class interest shifted to illegal drugs, about which the students knew more than I did. Using their first-hand reports, we classified drugs—by costs, effects, and dangers—and the students absorbed the *concept* of classification.

As interest in pharmacology waned, someone asked, "Why should a guy go to jail for smoking dope? It's no worse than a cigarette or a beer." "Yeah, but it leads to heroin." Does it?

Evidence? Should marijuana be legalized? The class voted. A slim majority opposed legalization. Should heroin be legalized? Unanimous opposition. How can drug laws be changed? "By breaking them!" Evidence? The segregationist law against riding in the front of the bus was undone by breaking it. They all knew about Rosa Parks. But traffic laws can't be changed by breaking them. What kinds of laws have been changed by civil disobedience and what kinds have not? We classified offenses.

Issues of social justice kept coming up. "Why do we always get busted for smoking pot and college kids get off free?" After heated discussion, I ask if they think it's better to be black or white. Silence. Then someone blurts out, "It's better to be black if you live in Africa!" A chorus of Yeahs. I ask why. A recitation of grievances against Seattle police follows. Much bottled-up anger is vented, some at me. When the storm subsides, I ask again, Is it better to be black or white? Are there any advantages to dark skin? Someone shouts, "No sunburn." When I supply the correlation between sunburn and skin cancer, the biological survival value of dark skin becomes clear.[34] An objective basis for pride in their racial identity is established: Blacks are less apt to get to skin cancer. Raucous cheering drifts into the hallway.

And then, out of the blue, came one of the best questions I've ever been asked: "Why isn't everyone black?" The speaker had grasped the essence of natural selection: everyone would indeed be dark if fair skin did not have its own survival value, at least in some setting. I didn't know the answer offhand, but I made it my business to find out before the class met the next day. My old biology text provided the explanation. And this time I didn't wait for the subject to come up again. It might never have resurfaced because asking it the first time had depended so much on context. Moreover, now it was my skin color that needed explaining, not theirs, so I had a stake in this.

The minute the class convened I told them about vitamin D, rickets, and sunlight. Reduced skin pigmentation—fairer skin—permits more of the ultraviolet component of sunlight to be absorbed, and this in turn enables the body to process vitamin D which protects against the crippling disease of rickets. Rickets impairs mobility and so it is a potentially lethal disadvantage to people dependent on hunting and making quick escapes. Animals that spend their lives in caves actually have translucent skin which permits maximal absorption of what little light there is. This is why Scandinavians, adapted to high latitudes, where there is little ambient sunlight, are fair.

But the downside is more skin cancer. That's why equatorial peoples are dark. Weather creates rainbows in more ways than one.

Apprenticeship with a Giant

How could a white man serve as a role model for twenty black teenagers? Well, a white man is nonetheless a man, so at least some of my problems were theirs and vice versa. But the truth is that I had help, crucial help, from a black man.

Not long after I began the class, a black adult who'd been patrolling the halls, watching for weapons and drugs, started dropping by. Charles Huey had no formal education but he had played some professional football. Huey, as he was known to all, was big and strong and street-smart, and within a few days we were teaching the course together. Sometimes we were joined by Huey's preacher-sidekick, John Little.

Huey added a vital element to the course and it wasn't just disciplinary. These students were in this class precisely because they had been expelled from all their other classes, so to expel them again would be admitting defeat. Anyone was free to leave at any time. If someone insisted in disrupting the class, Huey would tell him he had to leave now, but could come back tomorrow. Expulsion was never for more than one day, and the welcome back the next day was warm and sincere.

What Huey and I modeled for the students was twofold. First, we were a living example of a cooperative relationship between a black and a white adult based on mutual regard. Second, we took care to protect and affirm the young men's dignity. Students who must attend to the defense of their dignity have that much less attention for learning.

Huey, who had come from a home like those of many of the boys, realized the importance of involving their parents and families in what we were trying to do. After school we'd make home visits to see whomever we could find and talk to them about their boy's participation in the course. To give it legitimacy, we dubbed it *Science for Living*.

Driving to Garfield High School to meet my class, I experienced a euphoria not felt since my first year of teaching at Columbia. I was learning something from these young men that I'd never learned in any university—to bridge to another culture. I was also confirming my hunch that education works when geared to individuals' own questions, and proving to my satisfaction that neither they, nor my grade school classmates— nor I myself—were as dumb as we seemed.

I loved these students and they knew it. In one tense moment a vicious fight broke out in which two boys were throwing desks at each other. Yes, whole desks! The class moved in as one and stopped it—I couldn't have and Huey wasn't around at the time. From that moment on our class was a safe haven.

In another pivotal event, these boys solved the mystery of the prior disappearance of the school's audio-visual equipment, and handed it off to Huey and me in a midnight rendezvous.

We took lots of field trips. Sometimes I brought them into my world, sometimes they took me into theirs. I got permission from Boeing to take the class through the first 747 jumbo-jet while it was still on the assembly line. They took me salmon fishing.

Dumb Kids Not!

At the end of the term I tested my students and was astonished to discover that most of them had retained virtually *everything* we'd discussed—the generalizations, the principles, and the factual details, right on down to naming the four kinds of poisonous snakes native to America. They had done more than learn this and that; they'd had their first taste of mastery.

Everyone in the class earned an A (except one boy who, halfway through the semester, was shot dead by his father).

When a healthy brain is focused on something, learning occurs. That's all there is to it. The real problem is getting and holding a person's attention, which is impossible if students are devoting most of their energy to defending their dignity. When a student is inattentive, there is simply no point in continuing. It had always been true for me, and it was true for these dropouts.

After a semester, nearly all the students returned to regular classes with their first educational success behind them. They had discovered that they *could* learn, and furthermore, they knew that I knew and that Huey knew. The dumb-kid myth had been shattered and a new self-image—that they could be smart if they chose to be—had begun to take its place. Knowing that they could learn without sacrificing their dignity gave them agency.

Subsequently, many of them did choose to be smart kids. Follow-up studies revealed that once they returned to classes their dropout rate was considerably below the school average.

The problem had been attitude, not aptitude. Treat kids with respect and they'll learn. Humiliate them and they refuse. In our classroom, students felt they belonged. Once they dispensed with the carapaces they habitually presented to shield themselves from indignity, they absorbed the material like sponges.

For me, this closed the book on an early puzzle—the difference between smart kids and dumb kids. Years later, on a visit to Seattle, one of my students spotted me on the street, introduced himself, and told me that the course had changed his sense of who he could be and what he could do in the world.

By the time they joined my course, these students had actually reached the stage of open rebellion. I saw them as the tip of an iceberg that included a much larger, more docile group for whom schooling is synonymous with submissiveness not empowerment. Our two most pressing educational problems— why so many students refuse to learn and why so few who do learn are creative—are inseparable.

If students' questions set the agenda, the principal obstacle to learning—inattention—disappears and mastery becomes attainable. The secret to motivated learning is the secret to lifelong learning: sustained curiosity and agency. Everyone is born with curiosity, but in most it dies. More accurately, it's killed. Schools kill it with tedium, humiliation, and failure. But once their dignity is secure and their curiosity unleashed, students open their hearts and minds to learning.

An End and a Beginning

I never expected to find a new identity in the ghetto. The year in Seattle saw the end of my cover story as a physicist and the beginning of hands-on involvement with human, moral, and political problems. As if to signal my change of course, Ann had given birth to our second child, Benjamin Calvin, immediately upon our arrival in Seattle. Although we had known the baby was imminent, we convinced ourselves that Ben would stay put for the five hours we'd need to fly across the country. Fortunately, he obliged.

The birth of my starter identity had coincided with the birth of my first child (Karen). And the birth of my second identity with the birth of my second (Benjamin). I could see no connection between self-creation and pro-creation, but the timing made me wonder.

1. *Kindergarten, Chatham Township Public School, 1941, the year of Pearl Harbor. I am in the foreground, wearing a polo shirt, with my hands in my lap. Arlene is directly behind my head, with white barrettes, also with her hands in her lap. Our teacher is Miss Thelma Swenson. Two years later, in 1943, our second grade teacher, Miss Belcher, sent Arlene to the hall for having dirty fingernails. Arlene moved away from Chatham that year, and efforts to locate her have proved futile. No one remembers her last name.*

2. *Family portrait, circa 1948, on front lawn of our house at 42 Edgewood Rd. in Chatham, N.J. Father, Calvin Fuller (1902–1994); Mother, Willmine Works Fuller (1909–2001); Stephen Fuller (b. 1940); John Fuller (b. 1946); and me (b. 1936)*

3. Calvin S. Fuller at Bell Labs, circa 1954, the year he co-invented the solar cell.

4. Freshman year at Oberlin (1952)

5. Judd Fermi, son of Enrico Fermi, my close friend and mentor at Oberlin and Princeton. Photo taken at Cambridge University, U.K., where he was a researcher in molecular biology.

RÉPUBLIQUE FRANÇAISE

MINISTÈRE
de
L'ÉDUCATION NATIONALE

UNIVERSITÉ DE PARIS

ÉCOLE NORMALE SUPÉRIEURE
45, rue d'Ulm, Paris 5e

CARTE D'IDENTITÉ

n° 401
établie le 20.1.195

le Directeur de l'École Normale Supérieure
certifie que

Monsieur FULLER Robert
né le 26.10.1936 à
Summit (New-Jersey)
U.S.A.
domicilié à Paris 5e
45 rue d'Ulm
est
pensionnaire américain
à l'École Normale Supérieure
depuis le 1.10.1957

le Directeur de l'École,

J. HYPPOLITE

Le Titulaire de la carte,

Robert Fuller

6. Identity Card for École Normale Supérieure, 45, rue d'Ulm, Paris V. (1957-58)

7. *John Archibald Wheeler (1911–2008), who guided me through my doctoral dissertation (1959–1961), and got me a job at Columbia University (1961–1966). (Photo taken in 1984 by Beverly Spicer.)*

8. *Teaching graduate course on mathematical methods of physics at Columbia University (1961–64). Before the chalk dropped.*

9. With Charles Huey, who became my co-teacher at Garfield High School in Seattle (1967–1968)

10. First trip to Moscow (With Ann Fuller in 1968)

11. With Ann Fuller at the start of my second tour at Oberlin (1970–1974)

12. Officiating on a rainy day at a dedication at Oberlin

13. Karen and Ben Fuller, with Max the Cat, on front lawn of President's House at Oberlin (circa 1971)

To Bob Fuller
Best wishes
Walter F Mondale

14. With Vice President Walter Mondale and John Denver moments before the VP ushered us into the Oval Office for an audience with President Jimmy Carter (1977)

15. *Alia Johnson (1948–2010), on the Trans-Siberian Railroad, with Noah Johnson (age 1) peering out the window of our compartment (November 1978)*

16. *Noah Johnson (almost 5 years old in white shirt) and Adam Fuller (almost 3, no shirt) with Palestinian playmate in Jerusalem (April 1982)*

17. With Robert Cabot atop the Khunjerab Pass on the Karakoram Highway connecting Pakistan and Xinjiang, China (November 1986)

18. In Mogadishu, Somalia (October 1992)

19. With Claire Sheridan in the Russian Orthodox Church in Moscow where we were married (April 1995)

20. On the track in Edwards Stadium, University of California at Berkeley, training for the quarter mile (Fall 2000)

21. *After speaking on* Somebodies and Nobodies *to the China Club at Harvard University (2004). Both* All Rise *and* Somebodies and Nobodies *have been published in Chinese translation.*

22. *In Dhaka, Bangladesh for the publication of* All Rise *in Bangla (2010). The Chancellor of the University of Bangladesh, Arefin Siddique, is on my right and the Founding Director of Civic Bangladesh, Bayezid Dawla, is holding up a copy of his translation of* All Rise *on my left.*

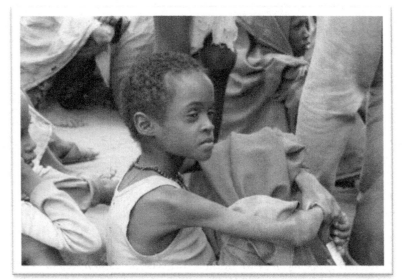

23. Girl starving during the 1992 famine in Baidoa, Somalia. Arlene is everywhere.

11 | Identity Inflation
(1968–1970)

How dreary to be somebody!
How public like a frog
To tell your name the livelong day
To an admiring bog!

– Emily Dickinson

From Asphalt Jungle to Ivory Tower

While crafting my "Farewell to Physics," and working with dropouts, I had put my ideas on education into a paper titled *Educating Model Builders*. Daniel Greenberg, my former Columbia colleague, was putting together a conference sponsored by the Jewish Theological Seminary in New York, and he invited me to submit a paper.

One of my Wesleyan mentors, William Arrowsmith, passed a copy of this paper to Theodore Lockwood, President-elect of Hartford's Trinity College, who was then conducting a search for his number two. The combination of Arrowsmith's recommendation and my views on education persuaded Lockwood to interview me for the dean's job.

Lockwood and I hit it off and he offered me the job. From the start, we understood our roles as complementary: I would vigorously advocate the reforms we both felt were necessary and Lockwood would remain above the fray, using the weight of his office to convince the all-white, all-male and decidedly conservative Board of Trustees to accept the reforms.

Our division of labor worked. Through a hastily improvised exchange with Vassar College, Trinity converted to coeducation overnight, becoming one of the first exclusive men's colleges to admit women. Within a year the average SAT score of Trinity's Freshman class, which now included many talented young women, rose dramatically. By the end of the year, the College had recruited many more minority students, faculty, administrators, and trustees; over-hauled its curriculum; and expanded participation in college governance.

President Lockwood's comprehensive, steady grasp of the situation kept me in check. By taking different roads to the same destination, we were able to fend off attacks from both right and left. Not often are intelligence, wisdom, and kindness combined in one person. Lockwood was the best boss I ever had.

At Trinity, my pattern of learning through apprenticeship continued—with Lockwood as mentor. I would save my questions, and then listen as he applied his broad experience and common sense to one intractable situation after another. One thing I failed to absorb from Lockwood, though he modeled it impeccably, was how to take the long view of controversial issues and wait out the opposition. Lockwood exemplified a patient delight in complex human problems whose messiness and intractability frustrated me. He played creatively with their intricacies, nudging first here, then there, all the while keeping his eye on larger strategic aims. I followed up, leaving nothing undone that might reduce the chances of success. Through my relationship with Lockwood, a tactical political mind was forming, much as a scientific mind had earlier in daily contact with my father, Judd Fermi, and John Wheeler.

Apprenticeship: Jewel of Education

My most important learning experiences had all occurred in the context of regular one-on-one contact with individuals. By asking questions, I could bring their teaching into synch with my learning. As question-asker, I felt in control, and I could stay with a topic until I understood it from all angles. Any loose ends could be tied up in a follow-up session. Questions and answers are the currency of apprenticeship, and apprenticeship is the jewel of education.

We usually don't think of our relationships with parents as apprenticeships, but with regard to our most fundamental learning—the acquisition of language, values, and the truth-seeking strategies we instinctively employ all our lives—they are the most influential apprenticeships of all.

Conversely, the absence of good parental models can cripple the young. What children need most to reach their full potential are exemplary role models they can imitate, an environment free of indignities, and recognition from elders and peers.

Malrecognition is as damaging to the development of the mind as malnutrition is to the growth of the body. In the twentieth century, we learned to spot and treat the latter. In the twenty-first, perhaps we will become as good at diagnosing, preventing, and healing the still unrecognized contagion of malrecognition.

As we mature we acquire *technique*—problem solving skills—through regular close association with more experienced and capable people. Such was my apprenticeship in athletics with high school star David Ford, in verbal skills with my dormitory mates David Thomas and Peter Funkhouser, and in problem-solving with Judd Fermi and Dave Larson.

Beyond methodology and technique there are osmotic apprenticeships wherein masters make students privy to their own creative process. Good mentors let us see how they handle failure and deal with setbacks. As in my apprenticeship with John Wheeler, some mentors help establish the witness in their students by unapologetically exercising their own witnesses in plain sight.[35]

In our early twenties, prideful barriers to apprenticing ourselves to others are easily overcome. But once you've made it in one field, ego can be an obstacle to getting the help you need to establish yourself in another.

Apprenticeship is no less important in building a new identity as it was in building the last. Every time I've fashioned a new identity, a mentor has been indispensable. But in one's maturity, a little mentoring goes a long way. We learn faster every time around because we get more skillful at zeroing in on just what we're missing. In one's forties and fifties, by posing just the right question to a master, one can come away with exactly what one needs to know to put the final piece into a nascent identity.

It seems to take most people about a decade to become passably good at anything. We're drawn to areas in which we sense the possibility of mastery. It took me about ten years to become competent at physics, and it took that long to complete my apprenticeship with Peter Putnam. It took me even longer to learn to write, perhaps because I didn't begin in earnest until I was almost fifty. But, as with my other pursuits, apprenticing myself—this time to experienced editors and writers—was essential.[36]

In the terminology of computers, it's as if each identity one takes on is a software program—an *App*—encoded in the neural net.

An expert is someone who knows most of the mistakes you can make in a field.

– John A. Wheeler, quoting Niels Bohr

Being Taken for a Somebody

During my second year as dean at Trinity, it dawned on me that I had done and learned all I could there. I was not interested in administering the reforms that the College had adopted. In many ways, it is better to leave the implementation of new policies to those less involved in the partisan struggles to adopt them.

I began casting around for another position, and Albert Bowker, Chancellor of City University of New York, put me into the candidate pool for the presidencies of both CCNY and Hunter College. I was eager to work with Bowker on what struck me as a historic mission to rescue the casualties of New York's failing secondary school system. His plan was to offer its ill-prepared graduates "Open Admission" to the City University, and then provide them with all the remedial work they needed to make a success of college.

When the presidential search committees at CCNY and Hunter opted for more experienced candidates, Bowker invited me to join him in the Chancellor's office and wait for the next available presidency in the CUNY system.

In one of our conversations, Bowker had described looking down from his office window atop the administration building and seeing demonstrations converging on him from north, south, east, and west. What's more, he personally felt the protesters' demands were legitimate.

Albert Bower's vision of education was the most ambitious I ever encountered, and he had political skills to match. I would love to have worked for him, but just then Oberlin began a search for a new president and the Chairman of the search committee, F. Champion Ward, came to Trinity to check me out. He concluded the interview by asking if I was interested in the job at Oberlin.

I told him that I was, but only if Oberlin was really serious about the educational and social transformation that was already sweeping the country. This was exactly what he wanted to hear and he set a date for me to visit campus and meet with the search committee.

The interview process confirmed what I suspected: under the spell of its own liberal mystique, Oberlin had been resting on its laurels. Throughout most of its history Oberlin had been a leader in educational and social innovation. It prides itself on introducing coeducation (in 1833). The literal-minded preachers who founded it had accepted at face value biblical teachings of human equality, so not only did they admit women, they also felt it obliged to admit people of color. Accordingly, Oberlin had long practiced color-blind admissions, but now, in the midst of a national crisis over race, where was my alma mater?

When I arrived on campus, it was with a sense of mission. My country was not living up to its ideals in its treatment of minorities, and Oberlin, where I had first taken those ideals to heart, seemed to me to be dragging its feet. Most students, a majority of the trustees, and a significant number of faculty shared the view that things could not be set right soon enough. There was widespread frustration with the previous administration's sluggish response to changing times. Oberlin now seemed ready to consider some far-reaching reforms, and if this was so I wanted to be part of it.

When it seemed they were about to offer me the job, I made a second visit to the campus to find out if there was enough faculty support to bring about real change. I could not take this for granted because Oberlin College was run by its faculty. The president and deans had a vote, yes, but only as individuals. They exercised no veto power over appointments and tenure, as at most academic institutions, and most importantly, they did not control the academic budget. Even faculty salaries were set by a committee of professors. I used to joke that at Oberlin the president had only one area of absolute authority: choosing the color of the toilet paper. The faculty governed everything else. Taking the measure of their opposition to reform was therefore of critical importance to the prospects for change.

Every constituency I talked to voiced its support for fundamental change—every constituency except one, the senior faculty. Most of the senior professors, whose support would be vital to reform, were cautious and circumspect. One member of the presidential search committee had characterized his colleagues as "reasonable men, willing to listen and to debate the issues on their merits." But, he'd warned, "Getting their votes won't be like shaking ripe apples off a tree." I thought some high winds might shake a few of those apples loose.

I don't think I'd have been interested in college administration at all if weren't for the national mood. As the sixties turned into the seventies, most of the reforms students were calling for were still unrealized. As it turned out, the reformist spirit of the sixties would last for the first three years of the seventies.

Oberlin's Board of Trustees expected me to stay for at least five years. Without any idea of what I'd do afterward—but knowing it could not be physics—I accepted the Board's offer.

Nothing on my résumé would have gotten me the job if I had not also been a tall white male. Image counts for a lot in choosing leaders. The signal importance of height struck me when, just before taking office, I attended a conference of academic presidents. Except for the fact that they were all white, it could have been a reunion of former pro-basketball players. Though I was six foot three, at least half of them towered above me. Especially among males, height confers a kind of rank all by itself, and lack of it can be a source of insecurity and suffering. A classmate at Princeton told of serving on a doctoral committee in which the chairman humiliated a short candidate. Seeing that the student had filled the blackboard within his limited reach, the committee chairman had instructed him to climb up on a chair so he could write his equations at the top. As a last rite of initiation, the young man was made to look and feel like a schoolboy. The chairman smirked condescendingly behind his back, and looked around to see if others shared his delight in the student's debasement.

At Oberlin, age, not height, was my problem. At thirty-three I was too young to be trusted by the faculty and too old to be trusted by the students.

All Men Are Created Equal—Rhetoric or Reality?

For a century Oberlin had held the high moral ground for its admissions policy toward people of color. But by 1970, college policy was under attack by students and alumni. Using color-blind admissions criteria, the percentage of black students at Oberlin had always been about one percent, higher than other predominantly white colleges, but paltry compared to the national percentage of African-Americans. The debate over this led to a consensus that economic and educational handicaps were the reasons that a lower percentage of blacks met Oberlin's admission criteria. We sought a way to ensure that more students of minority backgrounds would be admitted, but without imposing quotas, which were anathema because of their widespread use in years past against Jews.

The argument went like this: Oberlin has never had a quota for Jews. If we have a ten percent minimum for minorities, that implies a ninety percent maximum on whites.

What is that but a quota? Individual merit alone should determine admission, as it always has.

The battle to overlook the principle of no quotas, which had been a bulwark *against* anti-Semitism, and open the door to more black students, was fierce. Tempers were at the boiling point. Finally, we reached agreement to work toward *goals* for minority enrollment. The fact that goals functioned much like quotas—in that those who supported them were determined to meet them—was soft-pedaled. Within a few years the percentage of minority students in colleges around the country began reflecting their numbers nationally. I saw affirmative action as a kind of class action remedy to compensate African-Americans and other minorities for the collective discrimination they had long endured.

The hurricane that blew through campus during my tenure as president took a toll on everyone. Eighty-hour weeks were routine for me, hundred-hour weeks, not uncommon. When I wasn't at my desk or attending committee meetings, I cruised the campus talking to anyone and everyone. The men who stoked the furnace that heated the campus were astonished to see me, but delighted to explain how the furnace worked.

By the end of my tenure, many faculty and administrators were exhausted, and so was I. Together we had reformed virtually every aspect of the College's operations—admissions, appointments, curricula, grading, ethnic and cultural studies, interdisciplinary programs, performing arts, physical education, student life, the status of women, counseling, budgeting, and investment policy.

Oberlin's introduction of coed dorms made the cover of *Life*. A titillating photo of a male and female student holding hands surely boosted circulation that week. Sports journalist Howard Cosell reported a first on national television when the college made history by appointing black *head* coaches in football, track, and basketball.[37] The new track coach was none other than Tommie Smith, who'd gained worldwide fame by giving the black power salute upon receiving the gold medal for the 200 meter sprint in the 1968 Mexico City Olympics. Before we offered him the job at Oberlin, his defiant gesture had reduced the Usain Bolt of his era to selling cars.

For the most part, Oberlin faced up to the changing times and in fact reclaimed the leadership role it had long enjoyed. Applications soared. There was, however, one notable failure—governance. When the dust settled, Oberlin still had the same decision-making process which, because of its unrepresentative nature, had insulated the faculty from the social changes that were transforming the world.

About this time Switzerland was reconsidering its centuries-old policy of the exclusively male franchise. To no one's surprise, Swiss men at first decided that it was in the national interest that they retain their monopoly on power. Though I chided the faculty by bringing up the parallel with Switzerland, they likewise decided it was in the College's best interest that they maintain their monopoly on political power. Although the immediate causes of dissatisfaction had been removed, and the voices of protest temporarily stilled, paternalistic governance was left intact.

As it happened, the failure to adopt a more inclusive, participatory model of governance left me with a sense of unfinished business that would fuel my endeavors long after I'd left Oberlin.

12 | A Somebody Is a Once and Future Nobody
(1970–1974)

...the children's eyes
In momentary wonder stare upon
A sixty-year-old smiling public man.
   – W. B. Yeats, *Among School Children*

A Smiling Public Man

During my first week in office at Oberlin, a professor, twenty years my senior, had dropped by my office to wish me well. As he left he said, "Good-bye, Dad"—those very words! I thought it was a joke until I saw the expression on his face: it was that of a little boy. The words that had escaped his lips had nothing to do with me as an individual, everything to do with my office and title. It was an example of the same transference that had made it so hard for me to call Professor Wheeler by his first name. Transference is defined by psychologists as the redirection of feelings and desires, especially those from childhood, to a new object, often an authority figure.

Psychologists see the awe that people have for the rich, famous, and powerful as examples of transference. VIPs who are insecure in their status, can even have transference on their idea of themselves, revealing their self-doubt in their touchiness over how they're treated by subordinates.

Ruth Gruber, an Oberlin student, was either free of transference or determined not to be intimidated by the trappings of authority. She approached me one day as I walked across the Oberlin campus and declared "Unless you learn to dance your growth will be blocked. If you like, I'll teach you." She explained that she had noticed me at a party enviously watching students dancing to rock and roll. I showed up at her dorm room at the appointed hour and, with her coaxing and musical accompaniment from the Four Tops, I self-consciously danced my way out of a strait-jacket of inhibitions.

It was as if Ruth had finally given me that private singing lesson promised by my seventh grade teacher. The same self-consciousness that had prevented me from singing, had kept me from dancing. I think it stems from a propensity to stand outside myself as a witness from which remove I experience existential embarrassment. The feeling is one of sticking out into the universe and, like a tortoise under attack, I want to tuck my head into my shell.

Ten years after she coaxed me into dancing, I ran into Ruth in Warsaw, where she was reporting for United Press International on the Solidarity-led revolution in Poland, and we danced all night.

The flip side of undue deference is gratuitous defiance. To compensate for feelings of transference some make a habit of resisting anything that issues from authorities. Subservience to rank and habitual rebellion against it are both manifestations of transference. Dependency and counter-dependency constitute a double-barreled threat to mature rational governance.

My presidency at Oberlin coincided with Nixon's abuse of presidential power so people were even more inclined than usual to view officialdom with suspicion—a predisposition that I shared. But Oberlin's problems stemmed from the monopoly on power held by the faculty. When power is in the hands of one constituency, it tends to interpret institutional goals in ways that perpetuate its own status and privilege, and can be late to address the grievances of stakeholders whose views are unrepresented.

Even more aggravating than the climate of distrust that pervaded campuses during the Vietnam era, was that, as president, I had to repeat the same arguments and speeches, again and again, to different audiences. I should have foreseen that administration would not be exempt from my gold-silver-mud progression. Burnout was a constant threat. Staying alive, the supreme challenge.

Staying Alive

The object of travel is not to set foot on foreign land; it is at last to set foot on one's own country... .

– G. K. Chesterton

One thing I did to stave off administrative rigor mortis was travel. While at Trinity, I'd made two trips around South America and one around the world, all at the behest of Battelle Memorial Institute. Battelle was considering establishing a research laboratory in Brazil, and my mission was to check out the Korean and Indian Institutes of Technology for purposes of comparison with the proposed institute in Brazil.

In 1968 Brazil was under military dictatorship. When I got to the University in Rio, I was told that the students had been sent home and it was closed indefinitely. This certainly didn't auger well for a research institute, and Battelle decided against it.

When India's Prime Minister Indira Gandhi learned that an American had been inspecting the Indian Institute of Technology at Kanpur, she wanted to know what he thought of her "baby." Mrs. Gandhi had championed graduate science education in India, so when my Wesleyan colleague, the English poet Stephen Spender, who knew her personally, let her know what I was up to, she invited me and Ann to her office for a briefing. A limo was sent to pick us up, and for two hours I did my best to field her probing questions.

Her interrogation led up to one big question: How did IIT stack up against MIT? Happily, I was able to tell her that I thought IIT belonged in the ranks of institutions such as MIT. Mrs. Gandhi had arranged for a whole generation of Indian scientists to receive graduate training at top American universities—I'd had several of them as students at Columbia and they were outstanding. So, I could honestly report that with these young doctorates in leadership roles, Indian science was rapidly becoming world class.

Time has confirmed this forecast. Indian science and technology has played a central role in the country's development, and is now emulated the world over. Mrs. Gandhi's vision has been vindicated. It's hard to imagine more than a few world leaders, then or since, with either her grasp of science and technology or her passion for education.

At Oberlin, my travels continued. In the summer of 1971, I stopped putting off something I'd wanted to do since the war in Vietnam began: go there and see for myself.

I knew that Pierre in *War and Peace* had been changed by wandering the battlefield at Borodino, and I fancied that experiencing Vietnam in person would do the same for me. Ambassador Bunker, who got wind of the fact that an American college president was poking around, invited me to dinner at the Embassy and offered me the use of a helicopter to see the country. My daredevil pilot amused himself by swooping down to buzz water buffalo—while I turned white.

At a dinner in the Ambassador's residence, I quizzed many young foreign service officers and CIA agents, and not one of them thought America's war aims could be realized. A few years later, as the North Vietnamese occupied Saigon, I pictured my helicopter pilot evacuating our Ambassador from the Embassy roof to the safety of aircraft carriers offshore.

When I returned to campus, the students assumed I was an expert on the war. Their credulity enabled me to focus the righteous indignation of the Oberlin community into a constructive protest. Oberlin sent fourteen busloads of students, faculty, administrators, and trustees to Washington to meet with virtually every Senator and Congressman and express opposition to the bombing of Cambodia. While those students descended on the Capitol, others back on campus erected a mock Vietnamese village. A helicopter was hired to napalm it as singers from the Conservatory of Music chanted a Greek chorus. The spectacle was broadcast to the nation that evening on the *CBS News with Walter Cronkite*.

Travel can jolt us awake and cause us to see anew. When it does, it's a vaccine against dogmatism and an antidote for chauvinism. As we struggle to reconcile what we're experiencing with what we take for granted, we strip away what's arbitrary in cultural practice and edge a bit closer to the universal. Non-travelers are more apt to slip into habitual seeing and thinking. Even to cross the street in a foreign city, we must cease sleepwalking...or risk death. It must be admitted, however, that travel may also confirm some in the superiority of their ways. As Thomas Fuller observed in 1732, "Travel makes a wise man better, but a fool worse."[38]

Travel not only invites us to see the world with new eyes, it gives us an unaccustomed look at who is doing the seeing. None of the benefits of travel compares to the oblique glance it allows us of ourselves.

So, we do not travel to get away from it all. The bumper sticker— Wherever you go, there you are—has it right. Travel fails as escape, but it succeeds as confrontation—confrontation with our habitual selves that, deprived of confirmatory surroundings, may first stumble, but then find new footing.

In my youth, I traveled to grow up; at mid-life, to wake up; and in age, to stay on my toes.

Wild Times

My years at Trinity and Oberlin—the late sixties and early seventies—coincided with one of the most transgressive periods in America's cultural history—the Age of Aquarius, of sex, drugs, and rock and roll. Love affairs were as yet unconstrained by fear of HIV-AIDS, and, thanks to the pill, sex had at last been freed of the inhibiting specter of unwanted pregnancy. For a brief shining moment, it seemed as if the strictures of American Puritanism had been repealed.

As president, I would hear rumors of intimate relationships between teachers and students, but so long as they were between consenting adults, I did not regard them as the proper business of the College. In those heady, heedless times, it seemed as if students felt shortchanged if their education did not include an affair with a professor.

The creative arts flourished during those years. Against the backdrop of Oberlin's world class Conservatory of Music, a continual parade of artists passed through the campus. One such was Twyla Tharp who, nine months pregnant, performed a solo dance.

The Oberlin Dance Collective, under the direction of Brenda Way, gathered enough momentum during its formative years to take off and establish itself in San Francisco as a dance company and center known worldwide as ODC.

I recruited Herbert Blau, formerly a director at Lincoln Center, to head up a new Inter-Arts program. Among others, Blau mentored Bill Irwin, who became a distinguished actor, and Julie Taymor (stage and film director, known widely for *The Lion King*).

There were also early stirrings of what would become the movement for gay and lesbian rights. Two incidents stand out:

First, a phone call from a wealthy trustee and major donor, ordering me to fire an administrator who'd been detained by Cleveland police for engaging in a homosexual act. Here the bylaws protected me from the trustee's attempt to impose his views. I told him that before the administrator could be fired, he would first need to produce a majority of the Board to remove me from office.

Second, a contingent of gay and lesbian students, inviting me to attend what they billed as the first gay dance on an American campus. After trying in vain to concoct an excuse for not attending, my wife and I dutifully showed the flag. Afterwards, a professor who'd also attended let me know that seeing us there was the first time he'd ever felt that he belonged at Oberlin.

On a lighter note, I will never forget the recent graduate who stopped by my office and announced that she would like to perform a dance for me. To my blushing astonishment, she proceeded to strip naked and dance to the beat of the boom box she'd brought along. I've always regretted not thanking her properly.

Dreams of Anonymity

I don't want to go around pretending to be me.
— Philip Larkin

I spent my final months as a college president play-acting the part. Though I still behaved like a college president in public, to myself I seemed an imposter.

If status had meant more to me than aliveness, I would have used Oberlin as a steppingstone to a more prestigious school. By my second year in the job, universities were asking me to interview for their presidencies. Somehow, I knew that if I boarded that gravy train, I'd end up one of Yeats's sixty-year-old smiling public men. I saw many of my counterparts go this route.

Indeed, I was yearning for time to think, to compose myself, to make myself over. I had come to administration with the belief that the job was to redress faculty and student grievances so they could get back to their real business—teaching and learning. By the mid-seventies American society had reformed itself and was on a new course. Demonstrations were a thing of the past. Campuses were quiet again. People were turning inward, and so would I. After six years of jousting, I was ready to put down my lance and dismount.

Although the immediate problems that had led to my appointment had been largely resolved, I had not been able to win enough support for the fundamental changes in governance that would have served as a national model of participatory, shared rule, and rekindled my interest in the job.

Opponents of many of the policy changes the College had adopted were organizing to repeal them, and my continued presence was their principal rallying point. I realized that I was becoming the issue, and could best preserve what we had worked for by removing myself. After privately informing the trustees, I issued a public announcement of resignation, effective Groundhog Day, 1974.

Careful How You Take Your Leave

Only when we open ourselves fully to the assaults on our self-esteem that are inevitable when we venture to enact our vision; only then can we understand and even welcome the role of failure in the cycle of eventual success.
– Gordon Sherman

Through Ann's family, I had come to know Gordon Sherman. Gordon's father was the founder of Midas Muffler, and, by franchising it, Gordon had built a corporate giant. An innovative philanthropist, Gordon was an early supporter of Ralph Nader. He had a son at Oberlin's Conservatory, and when he came to visit him, he'd stop by to talk to me.

Gordon Sherman impressed many as a twentieth century Renaissance man. He was for the business arts what physicist Richard Feynman[39] was for physics—a personification of derring-do and originality. Gordon played the cello, cultivated orchids, raised Golden Retrievers, took wildlife photographs, wrote like Shakespeare, and spoke like Jefferson.

When I told him I was leaving Oberlin, his advice was to put as much care into my departure as I had into my arrival. Without quite understanding why, I took his advice and spent days composing haiku-like farewells for each of the fifty-odd people to whom I was closest.

On the eve of my departure, I read these aloud, one by one, to those who'd gathered to see me off. For my personal secretary Betty Price, I adapted lines lifted from Lao Tzu: "She who tells does not know; she who knows does not tell." I labored long and hard over something for the Secretary to the College, Stanley Ornstein, and finally came up with an epitaph—Just SO. To puzzled faces, I explained that in addition to pointing to the obvious—that only Stan Ornstein lay below the headstone on which this epitaph would be carved—it also acknowledged Stan's two principal character traits—he was notoriously meticulous and famously fair. The haiku was a triple entendre! Unwilling to wait for his tombstone, Stanley had "Just SO" carved into a stone that he displayed on his desk.

Gordon Sherman was right, of course. These friends and colleagues had seen me through a storm. I was leaving; they were staying. They would adapt to the change at the top, virtually overnight. I could see that some were already positioning themselves to survive the changes that my leaving would bring. More than a few were glad to see me go.

Twice, Oberlin had come early into my life. While most college presidents retire upon leaving office, I couldn't wait to start over.

Groundhog Day

Legend has it that every year, on the second day of February, the groundhog comes out of hibernation to see whether spring has arrived. If it's sunny, then, frightened by his own shadow, he goes back into his den and hibernates through six more weeks of winter. But, if it's a gray day and there's no shadow, then, counter-intuitively, spring is at hand.

My third grade class had put on a play about Groundhog Day and Mrs. Bahoosian had cast me as the groundhog. (This role, though mute, was better than my only other theatrical appearance. A decade later, in another silent part, the Mikado would ceremoniously chop off my head.)

It must have been sunny on the second of February, 1974 because when I awoke—a free man—all I wanted to do was crawl back into my hole. I was so desirous of solitude and anonymity, I gave no thought as to how I might ever get back in the game.

Take-Away from Academia

I left Oberlin running on empty, but not empty-handed. I took with me a fecund question that would shape everything I would do subsequently.

An article, then circulating underground, with the provocative title *The Student as Nigger*, had caught my attention. The title said it all: students, like African-Americans, were disenfranchised. Many felt stripped of their individuality, forced into subservience, and patronized.

Later, at Oberlin, the black, women's, gay, and student movements—coming pell-mell on top of one another— suggested that something beyond differences in color, gender, and academic rank lay beneath the racism, sexism, and disempowerment of students that had preoccupied the college.

I sensed that the familiar "isms" were all manifestations of a more fundamental behavior—one lacking a name—and that further progress against the distinct isms would require that we redirect our fire at this primal cause. It was not until I myself had became a target of such discrimination that I was finally able to identify it. I named it *rankism*.

The distinction between legitimate and illegitimate uses of rank—that is, between rank and rankism—opened a new window on the world, and I've spent much of my time since leaving Oberlin describing what I see through it.

I'd begun as a nobody, spent a dozen years as a somebody, and now, as I left my title and status behind, I'd soon find myself back where I began—in Nobodyland. My before and after status reminded me of the title of W. H. White's book on King Arthur, but with a twist. If Arthur was a "once and future king," I was a "once and future nobody."

13 | Sojourn in Nobodyland
(1974–1977)

I'm nobody! Who are you?
Are you nobody, too?
Then there's a pair of us—don't tell!
They'd banish us, you know.

– Emily Dickinson

Misgivings

I left Oberlin with misgivings about the way I'd played my own part within its system of governance. In spite of the constructive changes of those years, I felt something was wrong with the process. There was too much suspicion and ill will. I was liked by some but hated by others, and I didn't like being hated. As I reflected on Oberlin, I came to feel that though I'd helped the College make some overdue changes, I'd failed at another part of the job.

As the title suggests, a *president* is expected to *preside*. He or she must encourage necessary changes, yet always keep an eye on the fairness of the process and protect everyone's right to be heard. That's not easy because there are times in a social revolution when the best thing a leader can do is take an unequivocal stand in favor of emerging values.

But, I could see that there were advantages to dividing the two functions—impartial witness and partisan leader—between two people, as President Lockwood and I had done at Trinity. At Oberlin, I'd had both jobs but had done only one—that of prime minister. No one occupied the throne and the College had suffered for lack of a neutral head of state.

Re-education

Within weeks of regaining my freedom, I set off for a Japanese fishing village that had been featured in the *National Geographic*.

I planned to proceed on around the world to New York where Ann and I had imagined ourselves living after Oberlin. But, alas, we were no longer planning to live together.

By the end of our hectic time at Oberlin, it was clear that separation was inevitable. While I was travelling, Ann decided to quit her job at Brooklyn College, to which she'd been commuting, and remain in Oberlin. Oberlin was the last place I could see myself living. So, instead, I opted for Berkeley, California, where we'd lived fifteen years prior while I worked with John Wheeler.

There, at thirty-seven, living in a rented house, sitting on its only piece of furniture (a mattress I'd found curbside), surrounded by orange crates of books, racked with guilt over the break-up with Ann and living apart from my kids, I came to rest. Looking back, it strikes me as odd that I was then so unconcerned about the future.

It's a pattern: again and again, with hardly a thought for where I'd land, I've taken the leap—leaving schools and jettisoning jobs in a search for...for what? I couldn't say then; I suspect I began this memoir hoping to find out.

Writing my life has shown me that underneath my restless quests is a longing to belong. So long as Arlene can be banished, I can be, you can be. What has driven me and drives me still is the hunch that there's a way to organize human society so that everyone belongs. My personal watchword for a world of unconditional belonging—that is, universal dignity—is NOLO: No One Left Out.

§§§

During the six tumultuous years at Trinity and Oberlin, I'd read little that didn't bear on the task at hand. Now, I plunged back into mathematics and science, politics and history, and branched out into psychology and myth, religion and philosophy. If I was not to catch the same old fish, I knew I'd have to troll in new waters. I netted some strange new species, and it took a while to tell the difference between edible and toxic varieties.

I read Virginia Woolf—most definitely a new fish—and was startled to overhear Mrs. Dalloway talking to herself as I do to myself. Her musings reminded me of Fritz Perls's Gestalt therapy sessions, wherein he prodded his clients into unfolding their psyches. It impressed me that Woolf was practicing Gestalt therapy decades before psychologists.

I had participated in a few Gestalt groups while at Oberlin, and was astonished by what lay behind others' masks. To find out what was behind mine, I signed up for a variety of workshops. This was the heyday of self-help seminars and New Age therapies. The consciousness movement in California was as inescapable in the mid-seventies as the black and women's movements had been a few years prior.

At an Esalen seminar, I struck up a conversation with a vivacious woman named Alia Johnson. She had taken her first name from a character in the sci-fi classic *Dune*. I was disappointed to learn that she was in the company of another man. But before we went our separate ways, we discovered that we shared an interest in two questions: What is enlightenment? and Is anyone enlightened? I hoped our common interests might eventually bring us together again.

Looking into Enlightenment

California was teaming with seekers of Nirvana and gurus eager to show them, for a price, how to get there. More than a few political activists had replaced their concerns about social justice with a quest for enlightenment. I was skeptical. But I was also intrigued by rumors of a state of consciousness promising clarity of mind and vision. Before I could join in the quest, however, I had to find out just what enlightenment was.

I'd met quite a few high achievers in mathematics, physics, politics, and the arts, and I wanted to know if attaining enlightenment would help or hinder them in their pursuits. Since enlightenment was touted as a state of exceptional lucidity, surely it would elevate moral behavior and enhance intellectual ability.

To find out, I read widely and attended seminars, workshops, and retreats with teachers and gurus representing a variety of spiritual traditions, each of which offered guidance in the attainment of enlightenment.[40] I also got to know several gurus personally, as well as some of their advanced students, privy to what went on behind the veil separating the novices from the gurus. My experience with public figures, including myself, had revealed that there's often a gap between the public image and the private reality. I wanted to know how these presumed masters acted when they were not functioning as spiritual leaders to a group of credulous followers.

Getting a close look at a number of individuals who were reputed to be enlightened led me to conclude that, as with religion in general, there's a lot of hype in the enlightenment business. Many reputedly enlightened masters live lavishly and are served by devotees who meet their every need. Most gurus are treated like gods and hold absolute power over their followers. As reputedly enlightened beings, they're held accountable by no one; their excesses are given a pass. Of course, there were some teachers who, as far as I could make out, lived exemplary lives. But lack of transparency and accountability ensnared many spiritual leaders in webs of financial corruption and sexual exploitation.

If Everything's Perfect, What About Hitler?

One thing I took away from my encounters with Eastern religion was that its lessons on detachment could be a useful antidote to the righteous zeal of the sixties. The catchphrases of the day were: "The world is perfect as it is. Accept it. Surrender to it."

While I could see that letting go of one's own desires would bring peace, it would be the peace of resignation and appeasement. When I heard gurus say "Everything is perfect," I always wanted to ask "What About Hitler?"

The Hitler Question became a kind of koan—a paradoxical question that can't be resolved in its own terms, but only through a shift in perspective. Eventually, I realized that if everything is perfect, then so is my desire for change.

To my surprise, this perspective made me less impatient. It was as if accepting the whole picture, myself included, tipped the balance in favor of more collegial change. Here was the better way of doing things for which I'd been looking since the strident sixties. A puzzling experience I'd had in India during those turbulent years suddenly made sense. It had happened in the holy city of Banaras where I was visiting an old physicist friend from Columbia now teaching at Banaras Hindu University. He wanted me to meet his guru.

We had to duck to enter his teacher's tiny room on the banks of the Ganges. It was filled with the glow of candles and the aroma of incense. A little man named Lahiri dressed in a saffron robe treated me as if I were an important person, though I felt like just another tourist.

I'd come from Calcutta where I had witnessed hunger and starvation on a massive scale. Refugees from Bangladesh's 1971 war of liberation had been pouring into West Bengal, and Calcutta's streets were scenes of human degradation and misery.

What I saw in Calcutta brought back memories of depression-era waifs like Arlene, who had sometimes come to school hungry. I recalled scenes of famine from Pearl Buck's novel *The Good Earth* and Steinbeck's *The Grapes of Wrath*. Televised images of starving children in Biafra had recently been seared into our brains. My own modest experiment with hunger in Chicago lay more than a decade in the past, but once you've experienced the urgency of hunger, you don't forget it. The full horror of the Bangladeshi famine had hit me as I stepped over a tiny starving child lying naked on the sidewalk outside our hotel.

Asked by my friend to say something to his guru, I described what I'd seen in Calcutta. He listened attentively, at once moved and detached. When he spoke his voice had a tone unfamiliar to me—a combination of passion and compassion I'd not experienced before. He spoke of famine without guilt or blame, without righteousness or pressure. Before I left he had given me to understand that if what I'd seen in Calcutta bothered me I could try to do something about it—or not. Either response was okay with him; he only hoped that my response would be true to my whole life experience.

I knew America had helped end hunger in Europe in the aftermath of World War II. Why not India? In Latin America, I'd witnessed hunger in the favelas of Brazil and the slums of Peru. Why not there? Why not everywhere? That evening in Banaras I began to wonder what it would take not to stop the next famine, but to end hunger once and for all.

"What Do You Do?"

I spent the years immediately following Oberlin living off savings and a few consulting jobs. Ann and I, on opposite sides of America, drifted further apart, began new lives, and agreed to divorce.

Though our kids would shortly end up living with me in California, for a few years I saw them only during school holidays. At forty, it seemed unlikely that I would ever have a steady job again. All I could do when people asked me "What do you do?" was hem and haw, allude to the past, or exaggerate.

No one takes more than a cursory sniff at a nobody. Because you no longer have anything to contribute to their field, former colleagues assume you're washed up. They gossip that you've lost your drive and creativity, and wonder aloud if you ever had any. When you try to explain what you're up to, they listen only to headlines, and quickly change the subject. You sense that they're hoping you'll fail spectacularly to punish you for your intellectual promiscuity, and reassure them they were right not to stray from their niche.

14 | Trading on a Former Identity
(1977–1980)

Into the Oval Office on a Somebody's Coattails

When Jimmy Carter was elected President, I saw an opportunity to do something about hunger. A former farmer, I imagined he might give the ending of hunger the kind of leadership Lyndon Johnson had given the ending of segregation. Carter was advocating human rights. What human right was more basic than the right to eat?

Shortly before Carter took office, I'd seen a short film entitled *The Hungry Planet*, featuring the late folk singer Harry Chapin, long a champion of the hungry.[41] This riveting documentary spelled out the steps necessary to end hunger. I was surprised to learn that there was a broad consensus among experts that it could be done.

Fifteen years earlier, I had been struck by how President Kennedy's challenge to send men to the moon had galvanized the effort to achieve the goal. Of course, a lunar mission and ending hunger are very different. The Apollo program, like the wartime Manhattan project, posed a largely technical hurdle, and what political problems there were could be handled in house. In contrast, the challenge of overcoming hunger would require multinational cooperation.

Yet Kennedy's call had spurred us to realize an impossible dream. Maybe it could be done in a different realm. The requirements for ending hunger were even better known than those for a trip to the moon when that commitment was made. Since World War II, dozens of countries had eliminated famine, and where hunger did persist, experts understood why.

Only one thing seemed to be missing—the political leadership to commit us to the task. Carter seemed suited to the role.

But how could I get the idea to him? I had no job, title, office, or secretary. Not even a business card.

But I did have one good connection in Washington. An old college friend, Richard Cooper, had just been appointed Carter's Undersecretary of State for Economic Affairs. I figured I'd start with him, and flew to Washington.

Cooper agreed to present the idea to the president, and a week later told me that he had brought it up to Carter himself while traveling to a conference on Air Force One. I waited expectantly, but nothing happened. Evidently, the mission to end hunger was not a priority.

But it was still on my "List of Things To Do." I'd have to find another way to get the president's attention. While pondering my next step, I got a call from Alia, the woman I'd met at Esalen five months prior. Although we hadn't communicated since the seminar, she was still in my thoughts. She was passing through San Francisco, and proposed we meet for lunch at The Magic Pan.

I'm seldom later than five minutes early and was already seated when she walked up. Before I had even said hello, I saw that she was pregnant. She explained that the man she had been with at the Esalen seminar was neither the father nor her partner, that she was not in a relationship with the biological father, and that she intended to raise the child as a single mother. I wondered who the father was but didn't ask.

When I told Alia about trying to get President Carter to take on the issue of world hunger, she offered to help. Later, when I mentioned my dream of riding the Trans-Siberian Railway, I got the impression she wanted to go along. A few days later, I received a postcard from her that all but said, "When do we leave?"

The next time I flew East for the hunger project, I stopped in Denver to see Alia. Soon we were traveling together back and forth across the country.

Alia had a knack for putting ideas into words and the compelling briefs she produced came in handy both in getting to see officials and in leaving them with something they could use to get me to the next rung up the bureaucratic ladder. From the start, my goal was the Oval Office. It would take twelve cross-country trips to get there.

On one of them, I stopped in Denver for the birth of Alia's child. By that time she had let me know that the father was Stewart Brand, a man of many talents, already famous for having created the Whole Earth Catalog. Two months into the pregnancy, she had told Stewart that she was having the child and would assume full parental responsibility.

At the hospital, I was asked, "Are you the husband?" "No," I replied. "The father?" "No." "A relative?" "Not that either." "What then?" I hadn't foreseen this line of questioning and had no answer. Finally, because they were not going to let me into the delivery room without an explanation, I blurted out, "I am the man." With a shrug, the nurse ushered me in.

I had not witnessed the births of my two children with Ann, but since then the idea had gained currency that men had a role to play in the delivery of a child. I felt useless, but nonetheless was excited to be present. To see a child turn from blue to pink with its first breath is, well, breathtaking. As Noah lit up, it was like watching a light being dialed up on a rheostat.

My commuting to Washington, D.C. continued and within a few weeks of the birth, Alia and Noah moved into my house in Berkeley to hold the fort during my absences. It was becoming apparent that, at the rate I was going, Carter's first term would be up before I could suggest that he make the issue of world hunger his own. It was all I could do to get appointments with low level officials like the Deputy Assistant Secretary for Africa. Time and again, what stopped me was an interrogator demanding to know "Who are you with?"

Gate-keepers ask that question to screen out those without titles. If you're not affiliated with some prestigious institution, you'd better be famous enough not to be asked. What I needed was a celebrity to get me through the door. No sooner did this occur to me than one appeared.

In the mid-seventies there were few singers more famous than John Denver. When he showed up at a gathering in San Francisco where I was to show *The Hungry Planet*, I could see that the film affected him as it did everyone else. Before the evening was over, he had agreed to help.

As celebrities like Angelina Jolie, Bono, and Lebron James have demonstrated, star-power opens doors. I followed John Denver into the offices of Senators Humphrey and McGovern, Ambassador Young at the United Nations, and numerous other dignitaries. After they got Denver's autograph—"for my granddaughter" was invariably their excuse—they would listen to our pitch. At first, I delivered it, but Denver was a quick study and before long he was doing most of the talking.

Within weeks we had a meeting with Vice President Mondale, and, with no fanfare, Mondale simply walked John and me straight into the Oval Office for an audience with President Carter.

Carter was just as he was on television: beaming and unassuming. A fly on the wall would not have been able to tell who was giving an audience to whom. Seeing two of the best-known men on the planet completely star-struck with each other made me realize that even the high and mighty are not immune to transference. I worried that our message would be lost amidst the mutual admiration.

Word that John Denver was in the Oval Office spread rapidly through the White House. During a private tour following our meeting with the President, First Lady Rosalyn and son Chip came out to meet him. This was the chance I'd been waiting for. I pressed a copy of *The Hungry Planet* into Chip's hands, and extracted a promise to show it to his father. Then we were whisked off to the White House Mess for lunch. I don't remember everything we had, but I know the ice cream was the best I've ever tasted. Before leaving the White House, I somehow got access to a phone and put in "guess-where-I-am" calls to my mother and Alia.

President Carter, who viewed the film that evening, immediately instructed aides to form a White House Task Force on

Hunger. Within days the *New York Times* quoted Andrew Young as saying, "The most basic human right is the right to eat."

President Carter proceeded to create a Commission on World Hunger, naming Ambassador Sol Linowitz to chair it. I visited with Linowitz just before the commission began work and suggested that since we already knew what the final report would contain, why not spend the night writing it ourselves and then persuade the Commission to approve it the following day? Why spend months on formal hearings? With a helpless smile Ambassador Linowitz reminded me of something I knew but did not want to admit: the reason for the Commission was not to research the hunger issue, but to build the political consensus that would be needed for Congress to fund the mission.

Almost two years later the Commission's report confirmed the feasibility of ending world hunger and spelled out a plan to do so, but it was too late. Carter's presidency had been consumed by the Iran hostage crisis. An organization called The Hunger Project, which came out of this work, has kept the pressure on ever since, but the task of ending hunger remains unfinished.

Working on hunger was my first political experience in which there were no bad guys. No one spoke up in favor of hunger. Ignorance was the enemy. And war. War remains what it has always been: a cause of hunger and famine. Although my work on hunger had meager immediate results, the non-partisan educational approach it called for was good practice for the nuclear arms race that increasingly claimed my attention.

Are the Russians Martians?

If decade after decade the truth cannot be told, each person's mind begins to roam irretrievably. One's fellow countrymen become harder to understand than Martians.

– Alexander Solzhenitsyn

I'd first thought about going to Russia while reading about Marxism at the University of Chicago. A decade later, Ann and I had tacked brief visits to Moscow and Leningrad onto a European trip. In the late sixties, American tourists were rare in the Soviet Union. Hotel rooms were sumptuous, and bilingual guides were provided to explain everything, all the while keeping a close eye on their charges. I've always remembered one of our guide's explanations, for it lodged a question that was only answered with the advent of glasnost twenty years later.

I had asked the guide how mental illness was treated in the Soviet Union. With a shocked expression she replied, "But there is no mental illness in our country. Mental illness is a byproduct of capitalism." She'd been taught this and she believed it. My follow-ups failed to narrow the differences between us. Her explanation—and countless others that I was given—was either testimony to the power of Soviet indoctrination or evidence of an unbridgeable gap between Americans and Russians.

Disagreements with the French held little danger, but those with the Russians threatened world peace. Given my notion of truth—as a synthesizing model that reconciles all evidence and perspectives—I had never quite accepted anything that didn't also convince others. "Martians" were people you couldn't reach agreement with, even on the facts, no matter how hard you tried. Of course, it worked both ways. If they were Martians to you, you were probably Martians to them. After nagging at me for a decade, my Martian question was now calling me back to Russia for a closer look. I wanted to meet the people whose weapons could destroy us and see if it was theoretically possible to find common ground with them.

As a physicist I knew how the Bomb worked. I also knew the guys who'd built them, and the things they built always worked. It seemed to me that the Cold War, unless it could be stopped, would inevitably turn hot. As grandiose as it sounded, I couldn't shake the feeling that our very survival depended on the answer to this Martian question.

Intrepid Partner

Alia was the partner I needed to help me find an answer. Exploration was our bond. Within a year, we had married and I was trying to find the money to pay our fares across the USSR on the Trans-Siberian Railway. At Oberlin, fundraising was the part of the job I liked least. As a freelancer, I liked it even less. Yes, the project for which I was seeking money was my own, and that made pitching it whole-hearted. But, funders expect grantees to have titles and status, and I lacked all affiliation. Nonetheless, I hoped that by trading on relationships I'd made as Oberlin's fundraiser-in-chief, I might scrap up enough money to travel on a shoestring.

§§§

Thus it came to pass that four years after leaving the presidency of Oberlin College, in the summer of 1978, I found myself waiting near a dirty phone booth on the streets of Greenwich Village for a call from the foundation executive to whom I'd pitched my Trans-Siberian project over lunch a few days prior. Encouraged by what I interpreted as a reprise of our old camaraderie, I was optimistic that he would come up with a small grant.

Despite my changed circumstances—no institutional affiliation, no office, no title, no secretary, not even a phone— as a former insider I knew how easy it is for someone with the right credentials and connections to score a grant for almost anything. During my tenure at Oberlin, foundations had seldom rejected our proposals, and if they did it was apologetically and with a hint as to how to recast them for success in the next funding cycle.

As the end of the business day approached and the phone did not ring, it struck me: *I'd lost membership in the club. I no longer belonged.* It was then that I remembered Arlene. In the communities that defined us, we were both outcasts. It was not that the foundation executive owed me a "yes"; it was rather that he felt at liberty to break his word to phone me: I had become a nobody to him.

Of course, there's a world of difference between Arlene's banishment and my experience in the New York phone booth. Arlene had been defenseless; I had a car, a home, and a little money in the bank. Our circumstances were so different that it took me decades to put my finger on what they had in common.

After months of fruitless searching, I learned that the United States Information Agency sponsored American speakers abroad. When I inquired, the USIA proposed to send me through Europe to Moscow and on to Japan to speak on various topics in higher education. They would cover my transportation and lodging in the cities where I spoke, as well as a per diem which, stretched very thin, would allow us to break even on the trip. One year-old Noah would travel free.

I didn't understand why I needed an ally for this journey across the Soviet Union, but I knew I did. As it happened, Alia and Noah were not just extras; they were integral to the whole endeavor. Our idea was to go as a family, act as a family, and ask questions about war and peace that matter to families. That it was a family, not a solitary man, transformed the project into performance art.

At the time we made this trip we had no sense of being part of anything larger. We simply knew we had to do it. Before Alia stepped up, I had tended to procrastinate on such ventures. Thus, in the face of Ann's strenuous objections, I'd put off going to Vietnam for years.

From Paris, we took the train to Denmark where I spoke in Alberg, and then continued to Stockholm where we caught the overnight boat to Helsinki. In Finland, we waited anxiously for a week for the visas that would permit us to enter the Soviet Union. When they finally came, we boarded the train to the Finland Station in Leningrad where, in 1917, Lenin had disembarked upon his return to Russia to lead the revolution.[42]

In Moscow I gave a talk at the *USA and Canada Institute* on the inclusion of minorities in American universities. The Soviets also had a minorities problem—they'd chosen the topic—and their follow-up questions betrayed not a hint of Martianness. As was our plan, Alia and Noah had come to my talk and, just as I was about to begin, Noah required a change of diapers. Our hosts took it in stride, offering us a mahogany side table for the diapering, thereby further undermining the Martian hypothesis. Russian unflappability over what, in my own country, could well have been an awkward incident, emboldened me to bring up something that was constantly on my mind—the disproportionate Soviet losses in World War II. I thought that an acknowledgment of Soviet sacrifices, from an American speaker, might help open a discussion of the nuclear arms race. I began by saying that in almost every American town there is a little stone monument, usually in front of the library or the town hall, carrying the names of those killed in World War II. Most Americans know someone in their town who lost a relative.

Then I said that I realized the situation in Russia was very different. The odds were that everyone in the room had lost a close relative. I admitted that most Americans were unaware of this and that a popular television series narrated by Burt Lancaster titled *The Unknown War* was setting the record straight. My acknowledgment of the decisive Soviet contribution to defeating Germany brought tears to the eyes of several professors. Personal invitations and complimentary tickets to the Bolshoi followed. Subsequent discussions confirmed that these people knew war in a far deeper, more personal way than most Americans. If anything, they were more alarmed about the arms race than my countrymen. No, these Russians were definitely not Martians.

§§§

The Hotel Ukraine, where we were assigned, was Spartan and dank. The food was greasy and monotonous. Not only did we have a toddler to manage, Alia was pregnant. In a low moment, she phoned Pan American Airlines to find out what it would cost to turn tail and backtrack across the Atlantic. To our dismay, a world-weary Pan-Am rep informed us that the airline had decided that operating in the USSR was impossible. Pan Am had suspended operations, effective immediately.

Alia's response was to whistle. I could always tell when she was scared because when things looked their darkest she'd start to whistle. Her willingness to share the physical hardship and mental stress of this and subsequent trips was indispensable to my undertaking them. Those who validate our dreams and support us in pursuit of them are no less important than mentors.

We've Been Working on the (Trans-Siberian) Railroad

Make voyages. Attempt them. There's nothing else.

– Tennessee Williams

Once we'd settled into our snug compartment on the Trans-Sib, the trip across Russia was quite enjoyable. We had a samovar for tea, and although dining car meals were barely edible, the roast potatoes, smoked salmon, and chocolate offered by babushkas on railway platforms are among my fondest food memories.

When I recall Siberia, I think first of the stars. Nowhere are they brighter. Lake Baikal, the world's largest body of fresh water and home to the world's only fresh water seals, is breathtaking in its oceanic majesty. How ironic, that throughout Russian and Soviet history there have been gulags not far from it. Alexander Solzhenitsyn, who himself found Russians harder to understand than Martians, spent years in the neighborhood.

Although we sensed that in personalizing diplomacy we had stumbled on something, we didn't immediately grasp its significance. When we got back everyone wanted to know what we'd learned. I did radio interviews urging families to take their next vacation in Russia.

Indeed, wherever we went, Noah's presence had helped break the ice. "Citizen diplomats"—for that is what we began calling ourselves as our numbers mushroomed during the 1980s—make greater inroads if they leave their attaché cases at home and take their kids. Everyone we met on the train wanted to gush over Noah and, to his annoyance, run their fingers through his strawberry blond hair. Having him along was well worth the trouble of dragging two hundred disposable diapers onto the train in Helsinki. A few months after we got back to Berkeley, Adam, who had already traveled around the globe *in utero*, made his formal entrance.

Not long after Adam's birth, I was offered a position at Worldwatch Institute in Washington, D.C. by its founder and director, Lester Brown. As a young official in the Department of Agriculture, Brown had averted a humanitarian catastrophe in India by foreseeing a famine and organizing a preemptive intervention. He had since left government to found one of the first environmental organizations—Worldwatch Institute. My efforts to engage the Carter administration on the hunger issue and my foray into the USSR got his attention and he invited me to join his stable of world-watchers.

Our meager savings were almost gone, and I needed a job to support our growing family. We packed our things and headed for Washington—by train, of course. Somewhere in Wyoming, the train broke down and we were bused to the Denver airport. Better Wyoming than Siberia, we thought, where the stations were hundreds of miles apart and roads impassable. Although many things in the Soviet Union didn't work, their trains and rockets did.

Later, I would wonder if the Amtrak breakdown hadn't been a sign. Within six months at Worldwatch, I realized that I didn't belong there. Brown, as was his director's prerogative, set the agenda, and while initially our interests had seemed to coincide, we were soon at loggerheads. He saw the primary threat to humankind as environmental degradation and wanted me to write about making recycling a part of the public school curriculum. I saw the primary threat as ignorance and war and proposed to write about the nuclear threat and educational reform.

While at Worldwatch, I was paid a visit by three activists[43] eager to enlist my support for their campaign opposing nuclear power. David Hoffman was an organizer; Kim Spencer, an innovative television producer; and John Steiner, a networker and philanthropist. (His father and uncles developed and marketed the Bubble Gun and the Easy Bake Oven, and had left John enough money to do as he pleased. What pleased him was connecting people to further liberal causes.) As I made the case that nuclear weapons posed a far greater threat than nuclear reactors, the outline of a new endeavor came into focus.

Though no Paul Revere, I was increasingly concerned about the nuclear arms race. Nothing seemed more urgent than reducing the colossal ignorance that Americans and Russians had of each other, so I made a vague proposal along those lines to David Hunter[44] of the Stern Fund, widely regarded as the godfather of progressive philanthropy. David offered six months' financial support, no questions asked. Emboldened, I jettisoned my regular Worldwatch income for the vagaries of freelance fundraising. I had six months to figure out where my next paycheck would come from.

In the summer of 1980, two years after seeing myself as a nobody in the Greenwich Village phone booth, Alia and I and our two kids drove back to California. As we made our way across the country, I realized that in accepting Worldwatch's offer to work on Lester Brown's questions, I had lost my way. Both of our concerns were legitimate: the only thing that's as important as how we treat the planet (Brown's focus) is how we treat each other (mine). But our passions did not overlap enough for us to work together.

My time at Worldwatch showed me that I could no longer subordinate my agenda to that of a boss—even for the security of a regular pay check. With Alia's backing, I promised myself not to repeat the mistake of working for someone else—unless we were actually starving.

This time, too, our cross-country transportation gave out on us, but with a twist. As our old Toyota pulled up to the Berkeley house where we'd spend the night, it shuddered and died. It was as if the car knew exactly how far it had to go, and was unwilling to go another step.

15 | A Better Game than War
(1980–1983)

Humpty Dumpty

*All the king's horses and all the king's men, couldn't put Humpty
Dumpty together again.*

– Nursery rhyme

It didn't take long for the tradeoff between the security of an
institutional job and the autonomy of a freelancer to become
painfully evident. Worldwatch wasn't the first job I'd left
without a safety net, but I had never before been responsible
for so many dependents. In addition to my two kids with Ann,
there were now Noah and Adam. Karen was at the University
of California in Berkeley and, at twenty, was the eldest in our
extended family. At thirteen, Ben was finishing junior high in
Oberlin and living with Ann. He would soon be joining us on
the West Coast for his high school and college years.

By house-sitting in Berkeley, we stretched David Hunter's
grant to cover a full year. I was confident that if what we
accomplished during that time was useful, more funding would
materialize. At Oberlin, I'd discovered that whenever I'd been
able to convince myself of a project's importance—truly
convince myself—financial backing was forthcoming.

But, of course, there is a big difference between a sitting
president raising money for his institution and a former
president raising money for an idea whose time has not come.
Vietnam had left people war-weary and the idea of nuclear war
was not something they were ready to face. How could the
danger be made clear?

In the aftermath of the slaughter of World War I, French
leader Clemenceau summed up the public's changing attitude to
war with the remark, *War is much too serious a matter to be entrusted*

to the military. The lethality of nuclear weapons meant the death rate in a nuclear war would likely be much higher. Taking a page from Clemenceau's book, we updated his mantra to: *War is much too serious a matter to be entrusted to politicians.*

While driving West, it had hit me that the Bomb made us all nobodies. People felt too helpless to face it. The place to start, therefore, was with our fear. Only as the public learned to stare the Bomb down was there any chance to transform fatalism into activism.

Alia and I, joined by David Hoffman and Fran Peavey, named our attempt to shock people awake "Humpty Dumpty." The idea was to get people to confront their worst fears by involving them in the planning for the aftermath of a nuclear attack. In workshops, radio interviews, and later on television, we asked people what they would do *if* the bombs fell. We tried to get them to imagine life *after* a nuclear war.

Envisaging the consequences of a nuclear blast was a sobering exercise. What exactly would the police, firefighters, and public health officials do on "the day after"? Within a few years, a film with that title had been shown on national television. It made Hollywood horror movies look like tea parties.

We knew there would be no change in government policy until there had been a change in public attitude. *Humpty Dumpty* sought to create a *psychotectonic* shift. Our real aim was to rid people of the infantile conviction—originating in transference—that father knows best.

Although it was the prospect of nuclear war that had roused us to action, it wasn't long before we realized that the fundamental problem was not *nuclear* war, but war itself. Human beings were unconsciously dependent on war for identity transformation. No one gives up something they're dependent on, except for something better. Another quest was taking shape. I would spend the next decade in search of a better game than war.[45]

Motzu

War's a game, which,
Were their subjects wise,
Kings would not play at.

– William Cowper (1731–1800)

After six months in Berkeley, Alia and I packed everything into a U-Haul and decamped to a small town on the shores of Puget Sound near Seattle. I'd had my eye on this property for years. It consisted of several waterfront acres that my great-grandparents and grandparents had once owned. In the early 1940s, my mother had twice taken me cross-country by train to visit her parents there. It was as a nine-year-old at their home on Puget Sound that I heard the news that America had dropped atom bombs on Japan and the war was over.

When we learned that the property was available, we thought perhaps it could serve as a home for our work in the world. It was on the front porch of that ancestral property—looking west across Dyes Inlet to the Olympic range—that I realized that old Motzu had been 2500 years ahead of his time.[46]

In the fifth century B.C.E., Motzu was practicing a peacemaking strategy tailor-made for political activists in the nuclear age. Traveling through China with a small band of followers, Motzu went to areas of conflict and tried to negotiate peace. Centuries before Jesus, he preached a doctrine of universal love according to which all humankind should be treated as kinfolk. His logic was that we love and protect our immediate family. Why should this love not be extended to the family next door? To our community? To our tribe? To tribes over the hills? To the entire nation? To nations across the seas? To the entire world? It's hard to imagine a creed more applicable to our globalizing world.

Motzu's prophetic insight was of the kind that take a few millennia to sink in. He was proposing an alternative to the *predatory strategy* that our species had inherited from its ancestors and still took for granted. Also, in contrast to sixties activism,

Motzu did not take sides. Its lack of righteousness recommended it as a strategy for defusing the Cold War.

Of course, as American nationals we were a party to the conflict, but perhaps we could cease acting in our national interest and instead act, as had Motzu, on behalf of the whole. All that was required was a shift of our political identity from that of American to world citizen. As it turned out, there were plenty of Soviet citizens ready to re-orient themselves in just this same way.

I saw the Motzu project as picking up where Humpty Dumpty had left off. We would expand the Humpty group and, under the banner of Motzu, personally take the idea of non-partisan conflict resolution to the world's hot spots. Ordinary Americans would reach out to the Soviet people on the grounds that war is too serious a matter to be entrusted to politicians.

Sensing that the Bay Area would be more receptive to the idea, we returned to Berkeley.[47]

At just this time, a New York philanthropist named Joshua Mailman was organizing a meeting of people with inherited wealth on the lookout for new, creative ways to use their money. The nuclear arms race was high on their agenda. A few members of the group, which dubbed itself The Donuts ("nuts with dough"), and who were aware of the Humpty Dumpty project, persuaded their fellow Donuts to give me a hearing. On that occasion, and on many others since, John Steiner created invaluable connections and openings. His contribution to my work—as an ally and champion—has been indispensable, from Motzu to the present.

After gaining the consent of his fellow Donuts, Steiner phoned to give me the green light, and I grabbed the first flight to Denver, drove to Rocky Mountain National Park where the Donuts were meeting, and pitched the Motzu project.

Traditional philanthropists would not have risked money on reincarnating Motzu's itinerant band, but a half-dozen of these pioneers took a deep breath and sent me home with pledges that would fund our first few journeys abroad. More importantly, I had met several people who were not only willing to underwrite our personal approach to diplomacy, but who would themselves participate in it.

One Donut, Robert Cabot, travelled with me in 1986 to the refugee camp in Peshawar, Pakistan, from whence we departed to Xinjiang Province in Western China via the Khunjerab Pass over the rugged Karakoram mountains. A "real" diplomat, decades before he became a "citizen" diplomat, Cabot, who'd written a prophetic, environmental novel after leaving the U.S. State Department, wrote about our high-altitude trek and subsequent work in the USSR, and, in his role as a philanthropist, made other trips possible.[48]

In addition to Robert Cabot, the Motzu Project had about a dozen active participants.[49] In the spring of 1982, half of us traveled to Cairo, and from there, by taxi, across the Suez Canal and the Sinai Desert to Jerusalem, where Alia and I rented a small flat. We spent our days talking with public officials and private citizens about justice for the parties to the long-running conflict in the Middle East. Egypt and Israel had signed a peace treaty the year before, and there was hope in the air. But, as Motzuers, peace was never the proximate goal. Rather we regarded peace as a condition that would follow in the wake of dignity and justice for all parties.

From Israel, Alia and I and our two kids went on to Ireland where we were joined by David Hoffman, Kim Spencer and Evelyn Messinger. The trio was working on a television documentary titled *Thinking Twice about Nuclear War*. The highpoint of the sojourn in Ireland was an interview with the former Prime Minister Gerald Fitzgerald. The low point was invisible to all but Alia and me: wine, once her friend, was becoming her foe.

By the fall of 1982 I was in Poland, where the communist government had just declared martial law to combat the rising Solidarity Movement. Next, our family went to Kenya and Senegal where we continued to seek dialogues with government officials and opinion leaders. But the Cold War was never far from our minds. Nothing haunted people on both sides of the Iron Curtain like the specter of nuclear apocalypse. The reason we hadn't immediately returned to the Soviet Union, was simply that, for a long time, we couldn't figure out what Motzu could do there.

Back to the USSR

By 1983, both Americans and Soviets were coming to the realization that we'd have to do something to reverse the nuclear arms race. One of the most important innovations made by citizen diplomats was the so-called *spacebridge*, a live two-way television hook-up via satellite that enabled a group in the United States to see and speak with counterparts in the Soviet Union. Kim Spencer, who would soon be producing at ABC-TV, had pioneered the use of spacebridge technology within the United States and soon became a leader in its application between nations.

One of the first spacebridges focused on "nuclear winter," a probable consequence of nuclear war. Computer simulations predicted that there would be a prolonged period of obscured sunlight and plunging temperatures in the aftermath of nuclear war and that, over time, the environmental impact of this so-called nuclear winter would dwarf the effects of destruction caused by the nuclear explosions themselves.

In October, 1983 I returned to Moscow with Spencer to help stage a spacebridge that would bring Soviet and American scientists together to explore the nuclear winter hypothesis. Carl Sagan, one of the theorists of nuclear winter, was on the American panel in Washington, D.C., and the Soviets assembled a panel of their most illustrious scientists in Moscow. My job was to brief the Soviet participants on how to conduct themselves on television. As it turned out, persuading Russians to converse, instead of lecture, was impossible. Before exposure to the market forces of commercial television, they were constitutionally incapable of saying anything in less than fifteen minutes.

In both capitals, we held our breath for the first 43 seconds of the live broadcast, because the screens remained dark. After what seemed an eternity, the participants' images appeared and were sent back and forth around the world. The show continued for two hours. Kim Spencer and Evelyn Messinger and their Soviet counterparts, Pavel Korchagin and Sergei Skvortsov, had produced a broadcast of historic significance. With macabre timing, it had occurred on Halloween (1983).

This first program was not deemed commercial enough by American network chiefs for prime time broadcast. Nevertheless, reports, documentaries, and dramas on the effects of nuclear weapons began to appear.

One of the Soviet physicists had summed things up for the television audience, and quite possibly signaled the end of the nuclear arms build-up, by flatly declaring that a nuclear war between the USSR and the US would be *omnicide*—the death of everything. Three strikes against the Martian hypothesis.

With the broadcast of that program in the USSR, I had a sense of a magical completion. Five years earlier Alia, Noah, and I had traversed the Soviet Union by rail, raising the nuclear issue whenever possible, but reaching few. Now, the Soviets had aired the program across eleven time zones and the entire nation of over a hundred million viewers had watched it.

When, a few years later, Gorbachev rose to power, the producers who'd stuck their necks out by championing spacebridges, rose to positions of authority at Gostel radio. Overnight, they could broadcast spacebridges between high-level Soviet officials and American senators, generals, and others in the Reagan administration. Working the Moscow end of the spacebridges, I watched as primetime television programs anchored by Peter Jennings and Vladimir Posner were aired simultaneously in the Soviet Union and, by ABC-TV, in the United States. Phil Donahue and Posner co-hosted shows for both viewing publics. President Eisenhower, an early advocate of breaking down stereotypes through citizen-to-citizen exchanges, would have been pleased. Before the eighties were out, dozens of these links would bring together scientists, politicians, musicians, and ordinary citizens.

None of the things we did can be proven to have advanced the cause of peace and justice—in the Middle East, in Ireland, Poland, the Soviet Union, China, Pakistan, Afghanistan, Kenya, Somalia, South Africa—any of the venues we visited. But we were out there, in the faces of the official diplomats, and often underfoot. Our contribution lay in simply showing up and asking for a give-and-take in which we represented the public's (non-partisan) interests. The TV and print coverage we got helped plant the idea in the public mind that ordinary folks had a legitimate stake in international affairs. In our meetings with government officials and political leaders we urged them to see their role not as one of angling to take advantage of their traditional adversaries, but rather partnering to find common ground and resolve disputes.

I analogized citizen diplomacy in the context of the Cold War to the Freedom Rides through the segregated American South. Freedom riders, acting as if integration were the norm, had helped set in motion the desegregation that followed. Likewise, citizen diplomats, acting as if the Cold War were over, had given peaceful co-existence a face, on both sides of the Iron Curtain.

While acting contrary to a social consensus is rarely enough to transform it, modeling a new way can sow seeds that help precipitate its collapse. The Motzu Project probably had its most important effects as performance art: it was not our beliefs that mattered; it was rather that we'd taken the trouble to go to the Soviet Union and listen.

One organization that took shape within the context of Motzu is the global nonprofit *Internews*. David Hoffman, Evelyn Messinger, and Kim Spencer built this organization through the eighties and nineties. For many years, I served as Board Chair.

With the end of the Cold War, Internews turned its focus to training journalists in fledgling democracies to serve as a Fourth Estate. Internews grew to have nine hundred employees with an annual budget of $60 million. It has worked in ninety countries and in 2013 had offices in forty. In 2000, Internews spun off Link TV as a separate non-profit. Link is variously described as a global C-Span and "Television without Borders."

When a Low Profile Is Just the Ticket

Until the spacebridge on nuclear winter, I had thought that citizen diplomats had to be content with intangible results. That the most we could hope for was the possibility of a slow shift in public opinion of a sort we'd never be able to confirm. I likened the work to throwing a stone into the sea. Reason dictates that the sea must have risen, if only to make room for the stone now sitting on the bottom, but the change is far too small to measure.

There was no doubt, however, that television had produced a measurable change in the awareness of nuclear weapons and the consequences of nuclear war, something quite unimaginable just a few years prior when the Soviet Union had seemed monolithic, impregnable, and indissoluble.

Today, public (or citizen) diplomats are working in many countries on all kinds of conflicts. The goal is never to supplant professional diplomats. Concluding formal agreements and signing treaties is properly the work of government officials. It's rather the *prior* job—creating atmospherics favorable to negotiation—that is the work of citizen diplomats. Sometimes this takes the form of bringing officials together. Sometimes it means engineering a psychotectonic shift in society as a whole. Almost always it involves shattering stereotypes.

As we plied our "trade," it dawned on us that our lack of official status was not a liability, but an asset. Without official titles, we couldn't easily be pigeonholed and discounted. As free agents we could say things that government officials could not.

To do more good than harm, citizen diplomats have to be able to see different cultures, one of which may be their own, as parts of a larger whole that embraces both and compromises neither. Frequently this means suspending your identification with your country of origin and donning the hat of a model builder.

While identifying oneself as a citizen diplomat sounded a bit flaky to traditional funders, it did enable a good many of us to make a living, thanks to a few open-minded foundations, creative philanthropists like the Donuts,[50] and television. When people asked about our work, I often got the feeling that though they were nodding agreeably as I struggled to explain it, what was going through their minds was "spy." Even friends were skeptical, and, without an affiliation with a well-known institution, my parents couldn't convince their friends that their son wasn't simply on vacation. But as noted, our very invisibility advanced the work because it allowed government officials to take credit for any successes.

If there remained any doubts about resolving the Martian question in the negative, the advent of *glasnost* and the collapse of the Communist Party's monopoly on truth dissolved them. On one level the answer turned out to be so obvious that the question sounds even more sophomoric than it did when first posed. The story was simply the old one of a police state suppressing dissent and enforcing conformity through intimidation. In the aftermath of *glasnost*, Martin Walker, who spent years in the Soviet Union as correspondent for *The Guardian*, recalled:

> ... how surreal Soviet propaganda used to be in the pre-Gorbachev age. It was like living underwater, in some subtly alien environment, where words had different meanings, or in a parallel universe where everybody had been brought up on a rather different history.

The answer to Martian questions is that, if both parties are willing to keep trying, then eventually it's possible to find common ground—even regarding complex social and political issues. At least on Earth, there are no Martians.

Does this mean that people are the same the world over? Of course not. Variations in color, religion, language, customs, and cuisine are undeniable. But the proper response to such differences is to celebrate them. The French slogan—Vive la Différence!—takes on new meaning and new life. Intractable issues that might once have lead to war must and can now be resolved by doing what scientists do. They make sure of the facts and then create an explanation that accounts for all of them. It's called model-building.

Model-building itself was the better game than war for which I'd been looking. Following Motzu's example, we'd been playing it all along.

To exist is to coexist.

– Gabriel

16 | Quests and Questions
(1983–1987)

Mad River: Preview of Eternity

Just before going to Moscow for the nuclear winter space bridge, I'd had an eye-opening experience at the bottom of a surging river in northern California. I had attempted to swim a rescue rope across the Mad River, which had suddenly swollen in a storm, leaving David Hoffman stranded on the far shore. One end of the rope was tied around my waist, the other end to a vehicle on the bank. Although the river was high, the swim itself wasn't difficult—I simply had to start far enough upstream so that the combination of the current downstream and my swimming would carry me to the stranded party on the far shore.

As I emerged from the water on the far bank and stretched out my arm to David, the full force of the river struck the taut rope. I was hurled off my feet and dragged to the bottom like a minnow in a whirlpool. Looking up through ten feet of water passing above me, I waited for the people on shore to reel me in. And I waited. Nothing happened. They couldn't budge me against the current. For an instant, I wondered if this was it.

At first, lying helplessly on the bottom of the Mad River, I felt chastened. Facing what could be my final moments, and seeing things from my vantage point on the riverbed, the difference between life and death dissolved.

To my surprise, it seemed that death would differ from life merely in lacking the particular picture-show seen through my pair of eyes. Next, I saw myself as from afar, first as a speck at the bottom of the river and then as filling the universe. The last thing I remember thinking before my perspective suddenly changed was: *Being dead will be boring, but not fatal.* It took years to make sense of that one!

Then I thought of the living: my death would end the suffering that Alia's drinking was causing me, but my absence would be hard on my kids. Reverie ceased. I tried to untie the rope around my waist, but the knot was behind me and I couldn't reach it. I remember thinking, I'm on my own—the same thought I'd had as a teenager when I realized there were no absolute truths.

The first step was to get to the surface for one breath. I watched these thoughts flit through my head with a curious detachment. And then, with a love born of the picture show, I acted on them with fierce determination.

Suspended horizontally below the surface at one end of the rope, and looking upward through the rushing river, I pushed down hard and repeatedly against the water below me with my arms and hands. Slowly I rose toward the surface, until—miracle!—I got my mouth into the air and caught a breath. Sinking again, I repeated the process while the current swung the full length of the rope parallel to the river bank on which the other end had been tethered fifty yards upstream. Pushing myself upwards, again and again, I saw branches above me and managed to grab one.

Later, I learned that Kim Spencer, when he realized I had not surfaced, untied the end of the rope attached to the vehicle. That turned me into a loose fish with a very long tail, and made it possible for the fish to propel itself up through the water to the surface. No doubt, it was Kim's quick thinking that saved me.

Such experiences cannot be staged. Without loss of control, there would have been no sense of surrender, and it was that unscripted moment of letting go that placed me outside the picture-show. In such moments, any illusions that we stand apart from the implacable universe are shattered, and we are revealed as the once and future nobodies we've always been.

From Quests to Questions

From childhood, particular questions dogged me like tunes I couldn't get out of my head. This memoir is peppered with them. Usually, they did not present themselves in formal garb, and here I've left them in the sophomoric language in which I first heard them sounding in my head. The best gifts I've ever received have been questions I couldn't shake off. Not a few have ripened into the quests that have shaped my life.

In the years following the Moscow-Washington nuclear spacebridge, my peregrinations continued. I immersed myself in the philosophical-spiritual traditions in India and took a second cross-continental ride on the Trans-Siberian Railway, this time from East to West and in the company of my daughter Karen who had studied Chinese in college and spoke the language. We boarded the train in Beijing, rode through Ulan Bator in Mongolia, and on to Moscow, Kiev, and Budapest, where delicious pastries confirmed our return to Western civilization.

Over this period, two very different developments conspired to shift my principal activity from traveling to writing. One was the advent of the personal computer, which solved a problem that had always made writing difficult for me. As soon as I'd put something on paper, I would see its flaws and inaccuracies, want to change it, and end up paralyzed. But the arrival of word-processing software enabled me to make changes until I was satisfied. The role of word-processing software as a weapon against writer's paralysis has not been adequately celebrated. The computer, by enabling me to solve otherwise intractable equations, had given me my first profession—physicist—and now it was giving me another—writer. In time it would give me still others: blogger and publisher.

As I wrote about my experiences in the USSR and South Africa, circumstances forced me into the unfamiliar role of a day-laborer. After decades of benign neglect by previous owners, our Berkeley house was slowly rolling off a crumbling foundation. To limit costs, I worked alongside my general contractor, Toby Wells, as one of his crew. Not only did this experience show me the backbreaking effect of manual labor on body and soul, Toby also provided me with hands-on apprenticeships in the relevant crafts (plumbing, wiring, glazing, sheet-rocking, plastering, welding, masonry and carpentry).

To my surprise, I discovered that construction and writing had much in common. Both activities depended on breaking up large tasks into thousands of small ones. By repeating atomistic acts enough times you could create something that was more than the sum of its parts.

It was no coincidence that my stint as a manual laborer saw my principal focus turn from experiencing the world to analyzing it. Summers spent mowing lawns and washing windows at my elementary school had probably prepared me to grasp this lesson. But it was the spade-by-spade digging of a pond on a piece of country property and pouring a new foundation for our house in Berkeley that showed me the cumulative effect of many infinitesimal actions. There would be a lot more writers if all those who dream of telling their stories realized that a daily output of just five hundred words, kept up for half a year, is the first draft of a manuscript.

At the end of six months of manual labor, the consensus was that I'd be lucky to get $10 per hour as a laborer. Before taxes, that would bring in about $20,000 a year—which would have left my family below the poverty level. I empathized with the undocumented workers offering themselves as day laborers outside the lumberyard.

Once, after a twelve-hour day in humid ninety-degree weather, I loaded the truck with debris, drove to the dump, and was unloading when I simply sputtered to a stop. I had become dangerously dehydrated, more so than at the end of a marathon. To avoid collapsing, I lowered myself to the ground and just sat there immobilized, wondering how I would get up. An African-American man who was unloading the adjacent truck saw my condition and came over to ask if I could use a hand. An immense wave of gratitude rose through me and, with this stranger's help, I got up, we emptied the truck, and I made it home—never to forget.[51]

Sitting Still in a Room

I have discovered that all human evil comes from this,
Man's being unable to sit still in a room.

   – Blaise Pascal (1623–62)

I had always preferred oral to written presentations. Quick to sense incomprehension or disagreement in an audience, I could interrupt a lecture I was giving and address the questions that were causing people to stop paying attention. Or, when I noticed an ambiguity in something I was saying, I could go back and say it a different way. If word-processing software hadn't enabled me to revise as I wrote, I'd likely have remained a talker.

In April 1987, in the basement of our house, I began writing a manuscript that I called "A Better Game than War." I hoped the provocative title would jolt people into acknowledging their secret attraction to war, and our dependence upon it for transformation. The thread that tied the book together was model-building as a non-violent means of handling conflict.

In a series of unpublished manuscripts[52] written as the eighties became the nineties, all having to do with belonging and exclusion, I groped my way toward the organizing idea—*rankism*—that would give teeth to a moral intuition I'd had since childhood: that everyone belongs, that no one should be left out (NOLO). When I began writing, I never imagined that it would take fifteen years to turn my intuition into a theory, claw my way out of Nobodyland, and find a readership.[53]

As my focus shifted from outward quests to inward questioning, a personal crisis, long in the making, came to a head.

17 | Inward Odyssey
(1987–1994)

Alia

The stress of our itinerant life—camping out in friends' spare rooms, moving in and out of five houses in three states—had taken a toll on all of us. It is ironic that so-called peace work is often fraught with conflict within the families and organizations drawn to it. Alia and I often wondered if our attraction to conflicts abroad was not driven by a need to understand the conflicts in our relationship. At one of our low points, Alia gave me a card with an aphorism by the Berkeley poet Alta that read, "Let's stop hurting each other. You go first." That it applied equally to our marriage and the superpower relationship was lost on neither of us.

When we'd moved to Washington State, Alia had insisted on commuting to the Bay Area to continue working with a spiritual leader. Though she jokingly described her own role in the group as "Swami Mommy," her keen psychological insight and charisma had propelled her through the ranks until she held a senior position within the group.[54]

My fiftieth birthday was the emotional low point of my life. One reason I traveled so much during this period was to minimize the time Alia and I spent together. No doubt she welcomed my absences. Though there were still flashes of the brilliance and verve that had originally drawn me to her, those moments were eclipsed by troubles due to her drinking.

My marriage to Alia effectively ended on the day she accused me of lacking the guts to leave her. Her dare, which I subsequently came to see as an example of her talent for creative provocation, triggered the break we knew was coming. The shame of admitting to parents, children, and friends that my second marriage had failed had kept me in a relationship that was years beyond its expiration date. Alia was right. I *had* lacked the guts, and in goading me to stand up for myself, she had found a way to precipitate a change we both needed.

Almost from the start, Alia alternately participated in my projects and made fun of their grandiosity. Partly, this was a test to see if I could make my pursuits real for us both. Ridicule forces us to a more accurate and bullet-proof understanding of what we're doing. But derision is a close relative of contempt, and contempt suffocates love.

In 2009, Alia was diagnosed with ovarian cancer. Surgery and chemo, to which she submitted with her usual bravado, failed, and by 2010 she knew she was dying.

Shortly before she died, I spent a week with her and our two kids, Noah and Adam, at her home in Connecticut. She acknowledged the toll her alcoholism had taken on our relationship, and I acknowledged that her willingness to join me in my quests had made them possible and helped me find my life's work. Together we took satisfaction in recognizing what we'd accomplished together and what we had each done since separating.

Alia died, at peace, at the age of 62 on May 5, 2010. All who knew her felt that a hurricane had blown through their lives, and that they were the better for it.

Claire

Two weeks after Alia and I split, on June 9, 1990, I boarded a Pan American flight in San Francisco. As usual, I requested an aisle seat in the emergency exit row. In the window seat was Claire. That the seat between us remained empty changed my life.

Claire headed the dance program at Saint Mary's College in nearby Moraga, and from that base she traveled the world teaching, choreographing, and directing shows. We quickly discovered many things in common and talked until we disembarked in New York to catch different connecting flights—Claire to Prague to teach at Charles University, and me on to Moscow to witness Russia's rebirth.

Later, Claire told me that, until she noticed me checking out her legs, she'd assumed—because I asked lots of questions and listened to her—that I must be gay. Before parting, we agreed to be in touch in the Bay Area.

Having just escaped from a long, painful relationship, I was not looking for a partner. Neither was Claire. When we did reconnect a month later, it was without designs or expectations, at least to the extent that a single man is ever able to rule out the possibility of a fling with an attractive woman.

Russia Loves America (for Five Minutes)

In the summer of 1990, Moscow was an exhilarating place. Not since the U.S. Army liberated Paris in 1944 had Americans been made to feel so welcome abroad.

As the USSR collapsed, Soviet communism, long touted as the answer to capitalism, was revealed as a recipe for degradation, stagnation, and despair. The image of the planned economy that has stayed with me is that of a Moscow grocery whose shelves were fully stocked, but with just one item—plum jam. Thousand of tins of plum jam.

Although the question that had initially taken me to the USSR had been answered more persuasively than I'd ever imagined, another quickly took its place: "Why has neither communism nor capitalism delivered economic justice?"

§§§

With the end of the Cold War, citizen diplomacy seemed to lose its urgency. My last hurrah came in 1992 when, with Kim Spencer and a small TV crew, I traveled to Somalia to try to get word out about the famine.

When gunmen sprayed bullets at our feet, and then threatened to aim higher if we did not hand over the TV equipment, it looked like our mission was over. Fifteen minutes later we were offered the equipment back for a tidy ransom. After some negotiation, which did not work to our benefit, we reached agreement, got our camera back, and managed to record some video of the famine victims. Citizen diplomacy, as practiced in the USSR, had not threatened our lives. But in third world countries, it looked to be a much riskier business.

At the office of Doctors Without Borders, I met Imam, the Somali-born supermodel and actress who'd played the Somali woman in the film *Out of Africa*. For a while after returning home I worked with her and her rock-star husband David Bowie to raise awareness of the famine.

I'd seen Iman as a gorgeous cover girl, but was unprepared for the tongue-tying impact her statuesque beauty would have— on men and women alike. Aside from Taylor and Burton, I can't imagine a more charismatic couple than Iman and Bowie.

The most remarkable thing about Bowie was that in private he did not draw attention to himself. Dressed in suit and tie, the superstar took notes on our plans, raised thoughtful questions, and subordinated himself to the business at hand. He was the very opposite of the flamboyant personas that he assumed on stage.

Most of the famous people I've met leave me with the sense that they're merely pretending to accept their admirers as equals. Not Bowie. In private he showed none of the false intimacy or condescension that color most interactions with celebrities. Thereafter, I heard his music with new ears.

Iman had access to President George H. W. Bush, and may have influenced him to send the U. S. Marines into Somalia in the final weeks of his presidency. Early in the Clinton administration, eighteen soldiers lost their lives in the infamous *Black Hawk Down* incident. In any final reckoning, that loss should be set against the hundreds of thousands of Somalis who were saved from starvation by timely U.S. intervention. Given the horrors I witnessed in Mogadishu and Baidoa, the president's decision to stop the genocidal famine in Somalia may well be viewed favorably by history.

Mortality Knocks

When she wasn't teaching abroad, Claire lived in nearby Walnut Creek. Having finally escaped from a maelstrom of a marriage, I relished the idea of living alone. By good fortune, Claire wanted the same for herself. We saw each other about three times a week, and spoke by phone on days we didn't get together.

After four years of a relationship virtually devoid of conflict and angst, a routine physical exam in 1994, a psa[55] test and biopsy, revealed I had prostate cancer. I elected surgery and emerged unscathed but changed.

When I came out from under anesthesia, I felt as if I'd come back from the dead. Asleep, there's some vague sense of time passing. If I wake up in the middle of the night, I can usually guess the time. Even in dreamless sleep, there's a whisper of mental activity, like the motor of a car idling.

In contrast, the half-dozen hours that had elapsed while I was under the scalpel were empty and timeless. It was the only time in my life that my internal clock had stopped. All I could think to say to my surgeon in the recovery room was, "That was good practice for being dead."

Shortly afterwards, still in a daze, it occurred to me that I might actually *be* dead. That what I was experiencing—the doctor, nurses, Claire, and other sights and sounds—was merely a dream. But then, who was the dreamer?

Of course, there had been no certain way to distinguish life from a dream before anesthesia either. But I had experienced a new, deadly level of unconsciousness during the surgery, and it was that experience—of non-existence—that suggested that the self we mindlessly identify with is not what we think. Even though I now act as if my "self" endures intact through thick and thin, the macabre perspective resulting from the complete absence of self while under general anesthesia has lent credibility to the notion of selfhood as a time-bound construct.

In the aftermath of surgery, I imagined that I was rid of the cancer forever. It was not to be. Within a few years, my psa began an unmistakable rise, indicating that the surgery had not removed all the malignancy. Although I experienced neither symptoms of the disease nor side effects of the operation, the inexorable climb of the psa indicated that the malignancy was growing. Prostate cancer ranges from aggressive to indolent, and mine, while relatively slow-growing, was nonetheless regarded as life-threatening by my doctors.

In 2010, with a psa that had climbed to 20, I was persuaded by a radiation oncologist, whose recommendation went counter to the conventional wisdom—that it was too late in the day for radiation to be effective—to submit to radiation therapy. After 37 ten-minute treatments during the summer of 2010, my psa dropped to 2, and has continued to drop in the years since till it is virtually undetectable. No one can be sure the cancer will not reappear at some point, but I've stopped thinking of it as life-threatening. Months pass during which I don't think of it at all.

It's complicated, coping with cancer. Not only do you feel a sword of Damocles hanging over you, the disease is as yet poorly understood, so professional recommendations are often contradictory. Before I submitted to radiation therapy, I participated in several clinical trials and experimented with many alternative therapies. None slowed the progression of the recurring cancer. Initial hope would fade to despair, then blossom as I tried something new, but, time and again, touted remedies would prove disappointing. The uncertainty over what to do became as troubling as the cancer itself.

But cancer had one salutary effect. Immediately after the surgery, I stopped putting off writing about my experience at Oberlin. Before the incision had healed, I was pouring all my energy into exploring those times. And, in what felt like a Proustian moment, I decided that instead of hiding my nobody status, I would embrace it.

18 | Looking for Dignity
(1994–2003)

He was a kind of nothing, titleless.

– William Shakespeare, *Coriolanus*

The Nobody Book

No one likes to be taken for a nobody. To protect myself from disregard, I'd cultivated ways to pass as a somebody. Here I'm using the notion of *passing* as it was used by fair-skinned African-Americans who presented themselves as white during the era of segregation; or, as used by gays who choose to blend into the straight world.

But despite my efforts to pass myself off as a somebody, I woke up one morning and realized that I had again become invisible. I was back in Nobodyland.

It was then that I heard new words to an old slogan ringing in my head: "Nobodies of the world, unite. You have nothing to lose but your shame."

A slogan like that calls for a manifesto. I remembered Arlene in second grade, exiled to the hall for her dirty fingernails. I thought of Burt, the bully at summer camp. I recalled the tear-stained face of Jimmy, the local boy with Down syndrome. I'd never forgotten or forgiven a Sunday school teacher who'd intimidated us with threats of hellfire and damnation. The condescension of the staff at my parents' retirement home grated on me as it did on many of the residents.

Upon finishing a first draft of a novel set in an Oberlin-like college (which wouldn't see the light of day for decades), I went to work on what I thought of as *The Nobody Book*. Immediately, I realized that, at last, just shy of my sixtieth birthday, I was embarked on my life's work. Looking back on my life, it seemed to me that everything had been in preparation for this.

The Nobody Book argued that we are not defenseless against the abuse of people who outrank us. It introduced a new tool with which the put-upon and unrecognized could make their tormentors aware of how they were behaving, and, if they refused to stop degrading others, put *them* on the defensive.

That tool consisted of giving a name—*rankism*—to the phenomenon of putting and keeping others down. Rankism encompasses all forms of degrading assertions of rank (bullying, harassment, self-aggrandizement, favoritism, racism, sexism, ageism, homophobia, etc.).

The identification and naming of rankism moves the fight for dignity beyond the limited agendas of identity politics—which seek equity and justice for members of groups defined by a common trait—to the wider struggle for dignity and justice for everyone. Because rankism is the residue of our species' age-old predatory strategy, disallowing it would mark the advent of a new era.

§§§

While president of Oberlin, I'd sensed that there was a meta-ism of which racism, sexism, and the other familiar isms were subspecies. Why had it taken me so long to pick up where I'd left off twenty years prior?

Not until I discovered that I couldn't get out of Nobodyland did I fully understand how others are imprisoned there. When I overheard that voice in my head declaiming "Nobodies of the world, unite…" I realized that my best chance to regain a sense of belonging lay in identifying with other nobodies and figuring out how we could all get out of Nobodyland.

I made a half-dozen copies of *The Nobody Book* and foisted them on my friends. They all objected to the title. I was fond of it, but in the end was persuaded to drop it when someone pointed out that it was like calling a book on fitness *The Fat Book*. The working title notwithstanding, everyone wanted to tell me how they had been nobodied. I began collecting their stories.

As the anecdotes multiplied, I incorporated them into the manuscript, and new sections and chapters seemed to write themselves. I reorganized the material, printed a dozen copies, passed them out to a wider circle.

Their response kept me going. I wrote a third draft. A fourth. After a few years, I submitted the manuscript to several publishers. Most responded with boilerplate rejections. One head of a major house misinterpreted my argument as an attack on rank and wrote, "I'm in favor of rank, so long as I am ranked high." Another editor admitted the material was compelling, but bowed out on the grounds that "Nobodies don't buy books." My low point came when Norton, which had indicated that a contract awaited only the signature of the vacationing editor-in-chief, decided to pass. The phone call came just as Claire and I were leaving our hotel in New York City to attend a performance of *Cabaret*. The dark musical, based on Kurt Weill's *Three Penny Opera*—a portrait of the Berlin underworld between the wars—turned my bleak mood to black despair.

A would-be author has no right to a publisher. Nor do authors have a right to know the reasons on which publishers base rejections. An author may fault a publisher's judgment, but after all, it's their money and they have every right to invest as they see fit.

On the other hand, no agent, editor, or publisher should subject writers to scorn, ridicule, or the silent treatment. When a snide put-down is all you get, chalk it up to the insecurity of the source—the preemptive act of someone who has probably been a target of humiliation, and is trying to elevate his or her status by diminishing others. Pity their partners, kids, and pets. The phrase "kick the dog" is synonymous with displacing the indignation that builds up in people who must put up with chronic indignity onto targets that lack the power to retaliate.

If you don't have ways of keeping setbacks in perspective, they can destroy you. During my years in Nobodyland, I hit upon a few ways of bracing myself against rejection.

When your usual sources of recognition fail, you suffer if you don't have substitutes. Why? Because recognition is to identity what nutrition is to the body. Put the other way round, malrecognition is like malnutrition—it's a danger to your health. Taking steps to prevent this is the key to surviving chronic exposure to indignity.

Five Ways to Survive Nobodyland

1. The Power of Two

There are no words to express the abyss between isolation and having one ally. It may be conceded to mathematicians that four is twice two. But two is not twice one; two is two thousand times one . . . .

– G. K. Chesterton

An indispensible bulwark against criticism and rejection was Claire. Chesterton's epigraph applies equally to my partnerships with Ann and Alia. In all three relationships, "two" was indeed "two thousand times one."

You're not invisible to the world so long as you're visible to someone. Claire not only provided encouragement; she gave me feedback on everything I wrote and she applied her editorial sensibilities to *clarifying* each successive draft.[56] It was in interaction with Claire that I realized that everything we think or do is more accurately understood as co-creation.

As our relationship approached the five-year mark, Claire and I both felt it was time for a change. Though we were still living separately, we decided to formalize our partnership in the usual way—by getting married—but to do so in an unusual place—Moscow. After all, Russia had put me beside her on that Pan Am flight.

For a mere $200, I booked an entire Russian Orthodox church, complete with priest and cantor. We were married in April 1995 in a ceremony conducted in Medieval Russian, incomprehensible not only to me but to speakers of modern Russian (of whom Claire was one).

Since neither of my prior marriages had exceeded fifteen years, it was mutually agreed that this one would automatically dissolve fifteen years from the day we met—with no hard feelings—unless we both chose to continue. During that time we made another shift. My house was divisible into a duplex, and Claire moved into half of it. We each have our own space, but it's all under one roof.

We now think of ourselves as living together, but not cheek to jowl. Eight years after we made the move into separate apartments at the same address, on the fifteenth anniversary of our chance airplane meeting, we met formally at the site of our first date and agreed to extend our relationship "till death do us part." It's odd how when you don't force yourself into the traditional mold, it sometimes comes round to claim you.

2. The Internet: A Nobody's Best Friend

By 2001, six years after first circulating *The Nobody Book* among friends, I had accumulated dozens of rejections from publishers. It was then that an Oberlin math major, Melanie Hart, suggested creating a web site so I could at least *give* the book away. I hired her to design one, www.breakingranks.net, and overnight, there were thousands of hits. On a bulletin board, strangers shared their stories of rankist abuse and discrimination. Within a year, two thousand visitors had downloaded the free book. Not only did communicating with them sustain me, their interest was tangible proof that there was a market for the ideas that I hoped would persuade a publisher to take a chance on the book.

The internet is a whole new realm where the issues of belonging and unbelonging will inevitably play out. But, on balance, it seems likely to be for many others what it was for me: a virtual world where I could experience a kind of belonging when the "real" world wouldn't let me into the game.

3. Start Something New

Though they don't always follow their own advice, any writer will tell you that the best way to shield yourself from the disappointment of rejection is to begin working on a new project, even and especially while you're waiting for word about an old one.

While in limbo, I revised my novel and wrote a sequel to it that introduced another generation of characters and carried the story through the end of the twentieth century and into the twenty-first. Inhabiting a fictional world with your characters also makes up for some of what you're missing in the "real" one.

4. A Daily Practice

When the world refuses to recognize your offering, you can try harder or you can offer it something else. It's best to do both. Any regular practice—for example, gardening, music, chess, birding, yoga—will improve your chances of getting some of the recognition absent which one hardens and becomes susceptible to cynicism.

For me, running helped see me through years of public indifference and rejection.

When the marathon craze hit in the seventies, I'd plodded through the twenty-six miles along with thousands of others. But by the time I turned to writing full time, I had abandoned road running for the exhilaration of the track. To illustrate how a daily practice can offset the deleterious effects of malrecognition, I offer this account of the Quarter-Milers Club, which gave me a sense of belonging when nothing else did.

Once I made the switch from trails to track, it was not long before I was working out with group of seven men, all in their forties and fifties. There was James, a character actor in films, our overall mileage leader; Peter, who administers a drug rehab program, quickest out of the blocks and peerless rabbit in support of others; Steve, a sculptor, who alone among us achieved the Holy Grail—the quarter-mile in under a minute; Clive, a playwright and poet, who ran with unequalled grace; and Roger and Toby, both contractors, the former unbeatable at any distance over a quarter mile, the latter hobbled by work-related injuries.

We shared training tips and provided each other with the sportsmanlike competition needed to attain our personal bests. Examining my response to winning and losing in the context of competitive track provided me with an on-going tutorial on the difference between healthy rivalry and demeaning one-upmanship. Athletics are about more than fitness; they can also be a discipline and a practice. I think of sprinting as yoga in motion: it's as much about attitude as performance.

For most quarter-milers the one-minute quarter moves beyond reach in their sixties. So, I devised a more forgiving goal—run the quarter-mile (or 400 meters, which is virtually the same thing) in fewer seconds than your age in years. Run a lap that fast and you're a member of the Quarter-Milers Club. What's inviting about the Quarter-Milers Club is that each year you get an additional second to compensate for aging. As club founder, I chose to make the membership rules simple and forgiving: fractions of a second may be ignored. Thus, a 65-year-old who runs the quarter in anything less than 66 seconds qualifies.[57] Once you're in the Quarter-Milers Club, it's for life. There are no dues, meetings, or distinctions of rank, except that the oldest member is regarded as honorary president.

By the year 2000, having added weight training to my workouts, my times were slowly improving to the point that I was only a few tantalizing tenths of a second away from getting into my own club. Finally, just days past my 64th birthday, I broke 63 seconds and qualified for membership. Nothing I did during my time in obscurity did more to help me cope with the rejections that dogged my literary pursuits.

I wrote *Runner's World* to suggest the establishment of the Quarter-Milers Club, and they published the membership criterion in their February, 2001 issue. From all over the world, I heard from runners announcing either their membership or their determination to gain admission.

Invisibility to some is not invisibility to all. Seeking recognition in just one place is as short-sighted as restricting yourself to a diet of potatoes. Malrecognition and malnutrition are preventable maladies. The cure for both is diversification of nutrients.

5. When Nothing Seems to Be Working

There is no disease so obstinate that it cannot be cured by the drinking of two hundred cups of strong tea.

– Samuel Johnson

Never underestimate a nice cup of tea to heal wounds of rejection, to comfort a solitary soul, or to sustain hope that your next try will meet with success.

Escape from Nobodyland

With each rejection of the *Nobody* manuscript, my determination to be heard grew stronger. I told anyone who'd listen—from former colleagues still holding prestigious jobs to panhandlers—about somebodies and nobodies and the rankism that divides them. I learned to recognize that a certain faraway look crossing people's faces signaled that they wanted to tell me *their* stories. After they had, a not-common response was to suggest that rankism would be a good topic for Oprah.[58]

In 2001, my ally John Steiner passed a copy of the manuscript to San Francisco activist Bill Moyer (not to be confused with the journalist Bill Moyers). Moyer pitched my project to New Society Publishers, the publisher of his own book *Doing Democracy*.[59] At first, New Society declined, as had every other publisher, but a year later, then in the final stages of cancer, Moyer persuaded them to take a second look at my manuscript, and this time they offered a contract. A meeting was arranged in Victoria, British Columbia, the contract signed, the manuscript delivered, and in the spring of 2003 New Society Publishers, located on Gabriola Island off Vancouver Island in British Columbia, published a hardcover edition of *Somebodies and Nobodies: Overcoming the Abuse of Rank*.[60]

In the run-up to publication, an author seeks endorsements—known in the trade as "blurbs"—from public figures whose name-recognition might persuade the public to buy the book and talk show hosts to schedule an interview.

Blurb-seeking is a harrowing business, and it can be full of surprises. I very much wanted an endorsement from Betty Friedan, whose struggles to expand women's rights had been an inspiration. Through the good offices of a mutual friend, I managed to arrange a luncheon meeting. When I got to Betty's apartment in Washington, D.C., she acted as if she didn't know why I'd come, haughtily announced that she could do nothing for me, and left me alone in the waiting room. Aides rushed in to assure me that she'd return, and when she did I suggested we at least get a drink and some lunch. Over the course of a three hour lunch, during which she consumed one whisky sour per hour, Betty mellowed and I began to wonder if she remembered why I was there.

Nothing was said about the blurb until just before we parted. With one foot on the curb in front of her apartment, but the other still in the taxi, she said, "Okay, I'll give you a blurb. Get in touch with my secretary." I had what I needed— her name on the back cover.

A less stressful experience was my interaction with Studs Terkel. John Steiner had gotten a copy of the manuscript to his acquaintance David Dellinger, senior member of the Chicago Eight, and Dellinger had passed it on to Studs. A few days later my phone rang and as soon as Studs introduced himself I recognized his gravelly voice.[61]

"Have you got a pencil?" he asked. Yes, I replied. "Then take this down, word for word," and he proceeded to dictate a blurb to die for.[62] In a trance, I transcribed his every word. When he finished, he asked me to read it back to him, and once he was satisfied, he told me I was free to use it however it might help. My publisher put it on the front cover.

I had spent almost nine years rewriting the book before it came out. In the process, I discovered that Nobodyland isn't really a bad place as long as you're not trying to get out. You can concentrate there, and since you're out of sight, you're free to make mistakes, explore new ideas, and develop them until they're bulletproof. During the book's incubation period, I wrote over a half-million words of which about one in ten made the final cut.

With publication, I had finally put into print and into play my vision of a world in which no one is left out. I felt relieved of one burden and ready to assume another—the task of spreading the dignity meme wherever I could find a microphone. This was what I'd been unconsciously preparing myself for from the day Miss Belcher banished Arlene for having dirty fingernails. Sixty years on, Arlene was out of the hall, and so was I.

19 | Stumping for Dignity
(2003–2008)

Somebodies and Nobodies

Unless authors generate publicity, or hire a publicist to do it for them, their books are likely to be stillborn. Leaving your book to fend for itself in the marketplace is like abandoning a baby in the Serengeti.

After interviewing several publicists, I hired Jennifer Prost to get my baby on its feet. Months before New Society published it, she was soliciting interviews on radio, television, and in the press. Because she understood the book and had a reputation for integrity, Jennifer was able to secure several coveted bookings. My debut was to be a phone interview with a radio station in Albany, New York. On the morning of March 19, 2003, I was nervously awaiting the station's call when my phone rang—an hour before our scheduled interview. "We're sorry, but the United States has just invaded Iraq. Try us when the war is over."

Other precious bookings, on which the launch depended, evaporated. Nothing personal, they explained, we've also cancelled a Nobel laureate and Stephen King.

But early on, Jennifer had gotten me a break that every author dreams of: Oprah's *O Magazine* would feature my book in an article titled R-E-S-P-E-C-T. When the April issue hit the newsstands, the phone started ringing. As Baghdad fell, an interview that aired over NPR stations disseminated the ideas nationally. Before that show went on the air, host Diane Rehm, whose guest list consists mostly of politicians and celebrities, cleared up the mystery of why she'd booked me: "My son just graduated from Oberlin. What years were you president?"

Our hour-long exploration of my yo-yo journey from nobody to somebody and round again drove the book within reach of Amazon's top hundred sellers. Twelve cities and a hundred interviews later, the book had found its audience, and the twin notions of dignity and rankism had been seeded.

A paperback was published a year after the hardback's appearance. Several months later, *The New York Times* featured the book in its *Arts and Ideas* section, running a half-page photo of the cover art. For a few heady days, *Somebodies and Nobodies* edged out the current volume of *Harry Potter* at Amazon.com. In the aftermath of the *Times* story, the BBC aired an interview that reached millions around the world, including Ruth Gruber, the Oberlin student who had taught me to dance. And more than a year after the station in Albany had bumped me on day one of the book tour, it offered me a spot in prime time.

If someone *had* published the first draft, the book would likely have sunk like a stone dropped from a Boeing 747 into the Pacific Ocean. Horace's advice to writers is pertinent. Rather than publish your first draft, he recommends "putting the parchments in the cupboard, and let them be quiet till the ninth year. What you have not published you will be able to destroy. The word once uncaged never comes home again."

When the book was published, I heard from many victims of rankism who felt validated by having a name for the source of the indignities they suffered. Some readers offered their own take on the idea of rankism:

> *The author has given a name to something that has been bothering me for years.*
>
> *Rankism is the ism that, once eradicated, would pretty much eliminate the rest of them.*
>
> *Rankism is so ingrained, so common, that it's hard to even notice it.*

It's comforting to know that a lot of the insults I've put up with in my life are being experienced by people everywhere. I'm sick of being nobodied.

Two Questions I Get at Every Talk

Equality and despotism have secret connections.

– Chateaubriand, 19th Century French statesman

Rankism is abuse of the power inherent in rank. More colloquially, it's what somebodies think they can do to those they take for nobodies. Common examples include a boss demeaning an employee, a parent belittling a child, a teacher humiliating a student, a doctor putting down a nurse. Corruption is quintessential rankism; bullying is archetypal. All the familiar ignoble isms are subspecies of rankism.

When I've covered these basics, and open the floor to questions, the same two always come up: "Are you saying we should do away with rank?" and "Isn't rankism human nature?" Even if I've taken care to deal with these issues, they invariably come up again during the question period. When they do, you can hear a pin drop. Everyone is aware of human differences in ability and expertise and knows intuitively that differences in rank may simply reflect those in talent and experience. Do I mean to deny this? And second, everyone has been both a victim and a perpetrator of rankism and finds it hard to believe that this impulse is not written in our genes.

The error imputed to me in the first question was also made by *The New York Times*. The headline over its piece on *Somebodies and Nobodies* read: *Tilting at Windbags: A Crusade Against Rank.* While it's a fair guess that windbags are rankist, the book, far from crusading against rank, actually validates it—so long as it has been fairly earned, signifies relative excellence, and rank-holders take care to respect their subordinates' dignity.

People have trouble with the distinction between rank and rankism precisely because rank is so commonly abused that most people jump to the conclusion that the way to protect ourselves against its misuse is to abolish it. This makes no more sense than solving racial problems by eliminating one or more races, or addressing gender issues by eliminating one of the sexes. What I've seen of communist societies and egalitarian cults tells me that eliminating rank is a recipe for stagnation if not tyranny.

In my talks I explain that, when earned and used properly, rank can be a useful organizational tool for fostering cooperation and getting things done. I had admired my boss at Trinity College, President Lockwood, for his exemplary use of presidential power. Like all effective leaders, Lockwood saw himself as a servant. George Washington set a high standard with his refusal to set himself above the people as their king. His rejection of the crown had been a defining moment, not just in the history of the United States, but in the history of governance.

When I compete in a footrace, I'm reminded that being outrun and outranked entails no shame or loss of self-respect. On the contrary, competition helps me get the best out of myself. Of course, if a runner who comes in ahead sneers at me that's another thing. Indignity breeds indignation—between individuals, groups, and nations.

What about the second question? Audiences rightly sense that the prospects for building a dignitarian society rest on whether the impulse to put others down is an indelible fact of human nature. The dignitarian vision will clearly be unobtainable unless it's possible to reprogram ourselves.

No one can be faulted for assuming that rankism is a fixture of human behavior. Just read the paper: rankism is ubiquitous, as racism and sexism were in my youth. But right there, under our noses, is the key. Just a half-century ago, all the familiar isms were regarded as immutable elements of human nature, yet with every passing decade these behaviors are losing legitimacy. The impulse to put and hold others down is undeniably part of our history, but it does not have to be part of our future.

Another way to put this is that our species is replacing the age-old strategy of opportunistic predation, which, admittedly, has gotten us this far, with a dignitarian strategy that will predominate in the centuries to come.[63]

Instead of arguing the point abstractly, though, I usually invoke some personal ancestral history, history that I know is shared by virtually everyone in the room.

My grandparents and their parents (who lived through the Civil War) were overtly racist. My parents absorbed some racist attitudes, but they did not use the N-word, at least not in front of me and my brothers. Accordingly, we did not have to unlearn it when, during the 1960s, it fell into disuse as part of the larger shift from a segregated to a multicultural America.

Most people of my generation—black and white—will admit to harboring residual racist and sexist attitudes. Yet most of us have learned not to indulge in racist or sexist behaviors. My four children show no signs of racism and have all dated interracially. And their children, my grandchildren, are of mixed race, and wonder what all the fuss was about. Of course, racism still exists. There's never a day that it's not in the news. But, we've come a long way since "Whites Only" signs were taken for granted.

While an American president of mixed race was unimaginable fifty, or even fifteen, years prior, it became a reality in 2008 with the election of Barack Obama. The moral is that it seems to take human beings five or six generations to reprogram themselves on issues of belonging—that is, to create a new consensus on who belongs and who doesn't. And if racism and the other ignoble isms are not immutable behaviors, then it's very unlikely that their generalization—rankism—is either. Rather, we'll discover that it's a relic of the predatory era and has no place in the emerging dignitarian one.

The barrier to a world based on the proposition "equal dignity for all" lies in our software (our "menome,"[64] that is our behavioral programming), not our hardware (our genome, that is our DNA). Judging from the timelines involved in overcoming putdowns based on color, gender, and sexual orientation, it's not implausible—barring a major setback due to natural or man-made catastrophes—that somewhere during the present century, we will raise our sights from the specific isms to the one that underpins them all. Once we consistently target rankism, it will probably take several generations to disallow it. Moreover, every step we take toward universalizing dignity will reduce the likelihood of man-made catastrophes, most of which can be traced to retribution for past indignities and humiliations.

On the Road

In the years following publication of *Somebodies and Nobodies*, I participated in hundreds of events and media interviews and spoke at scores of schools, colleges and universities. Along with Horace's advice to let manuscripts ripen for nine years, I would suggest that authors spend a few more arguing their thesis in public before publishing a sequel.

During that time, I got an ear-full. Anyone who has perused a book feels entitled to express an opinion about it, and readers, even those who've done little more than read the flyleaf, can be blunt. Gratitude and appreciation are nice, but you learn most from your critics. They not only point out the shortcomings of your book, they tell you what they expect from your next one.

I learned that there *is* an iceberg of indignation out there, and we've seen only its tip. Below the waterline is the bottled-up resentment of millions who are nobodied every day. I heard from kids, parents, teachers, nurses, physicians, employees, managers, and professionals of every stripe. The impotent rage felt by most targets of rankism exacts a toll on their health and happiness and thus on creativity and productivity. The situation is reminiscent of the bottled-up resentment of African-Americans living under Jim Crow. "Nobody" is the new N-word.

The goal of *Somebodies and Nobodies* was to diagnose and pin a name on the disorder of rankism and identify it as the principal source of manmade indignity. But no sooner is an illness identified, than people demand a cure. They also wanted a blueprint for building dignitarian institutions.

In response, I wrote *All Rise: Somebodies, Nobodies, and the Politics of Dignity*, published in 2006. Robust sales of *Somebodies and Nobodies* made finding a publisher for the sequel relatively easy.

Promoting these books has taken me to more than thirty American states, most of Canada's provinces, and to France, Australia, New Zealand, India,[65]Bangladesh,[66]and China.[67]

Although the long-term trend toward ever more dignitarian relationships and institutions is clear to me, I know it's far from obvious. The news, local and international, is replete with everything from rape to genocide. But despite the drumbeat of horrors, I think that many forms of rankism are on notice and in decline. I believe Martin Luther King, Jr. was right when he said: *The arc of the moral universe is long but it bends towards justice.* In support of his counter-intuitive long-term optimism, I wrote an article that aims to provide a theoretical explanation of why he's right and posted it as a blog at the Huffington Post.[68]

I've also tried to present the argument for dignity in a more traditional religious framework. As discussed in *All Rise*, world religions have long championed individual dignity, and served as its defenders of last resort. It seemed to me that the spread of secularism might incline religiously minded folks, on the lookout for ways to revitalize their mission, to throw their weight behind the nascent Dignity Movement as, after much soul-searching, they got behind the Civil Rights Movement. Toward that goal I published a short book titled *Religion and Science: A Beautiful Friendship?*[69]

In 2013, almost twenty years after I began composing the story of Easter Blue and Rowan Ellway, I published *The Rowan Tree: A Novel.* Over that time period, many of the ideas in my writings on dignity and rankism were explored, intermittently, in the unfettered realm of the imagination. Fiction shows; nonfiction explains. Often the two genres are complementary and mutually illuminating. They certainly were for me.

In both public talks and in the blogosphere, my arguments invariably meet with skepticism and cynicism from people who invoke the headlines to show that things are hopeless. Yet, President Obama invokes the notion of dignity in virtually every speech, and *Dignity Now!* is the common demand and rallying cry of uprisings against authoritarian regimes from North Africa to the Middle East.

Despite ebbs and flows, I believe that a dignitarian tide is rising. No matter how long it takes to envelop the globe, my life has derived meaning from trying to answer the questions *Who belongs?, Who doesn't?,* and *How come?*

20 | Nobodies Liberation
(2008–)

Be kind, for everyone you meet is fighting a great battle.
— Philo of Alexandria

Somebodies and Nobodies Live Happily Ever After

Our tickets to dignity are our identities. It took me about twenty-five years to construct my starter identity, which was modeled after my father's. I expected to be a scientist for life like him. But no sooner had I donned that suit of clothes than I realized it didn't fit.

For almost a decade, I passed as a physicist while putting together a new Bob, one that partook of my mother's activism, but was grounded in my father's empiricism. In my new set of clothes, I was again seen as a somebody for almost a decade. But then I withdrew and, not surprisingly, soon found myself in Nobodyland.

With the publication of *Somebodies and Nobodies*, I saw a pattern. On the road, giving talks and interviews, I had left Nobodyland and was again seen as a somebody. I began to think of myself not as a somebody or a nobody, but rather as a home for both as they took turns spelling each other.

I used to feel that being a nobody was cause for shame, but now I see anonymity as a natural part of the life cycle of any questing person. I regard "nobody" phases as time-outs during which new ideas may take shape that will give my "somebody-in-waiting" something to contribute. Nobodies create behind the scenes; somebodies perform on stage. Public recognition properly goes to the actor, but if he has any sense, he privately acknowledges the nobody who gave him his lines.

I suspect that potential somebodies and nobodies co-exist within most of us. To remain productive, we should give them both their due. If I'm unwilling to get offstage, I turn into a statue who can do little more than impersonate a former self. But without an occasional stint as a somebody, I lose my connection to others and my place in the game. Too long on the sidelines, and I show symptoms of malrecognition—grumpiness, resentment, cynicism. Empathy and love come more easily to the well-recognized, and may desert those who soldier on in obscurity.

Making peace between my inner somebody and nobody showed me that they are not antagonistic but complementary. Our interior nobodies, who create new material for our outward-facing somebodies, are indispensible to self-renewal.

Similarly, on the societal level, those whom we take for nobodies are indispensible to *communal* growth. To paraphrase Simon Leys, "Somebodies adapt themselves to the world. Nobodies persist in trying to adapt the world to themselves. Therefore all progress depends on the nobodies."[70]

Neither within us nor around us is there anyone who deserves to be dismissed as a nobody.

In the past, we've rationed belonging, granting it to somebodies and denying it to nobodies. As the somebody-nobody distinction fades, belonging becomes less conditional, dignity more universal.

As Iris Murdoch said, "Man is a creature who makes pictures of himself and then comes to resemble the picture." My life quest culminated in a picture long-prophesied that's only now coming into focus—a picture of universal dignity and unconditional belonging. If Murdock is right, then, ineluctably, we will come to resemble the picture.

Parting Questions

Quests have a way of generating new questions. Here are some questions that are alive for me:

- What would life be like if belonging were unconditional and dignity secure?
- What are the political implications of recognizing that the selves we field are not our sole creations, but rather co-

creations? That it takes a community to do anything (including writing a book).

- What form of governance would support and sustain universal dignity?
- How will human identity be affected by the advent of machines that work the same way brains do but are more intelligent and creative than humans?[71]
- Will we eventually harness enough of Nature's power to travel to other solar systems, redesign the galaxy, and perhaps even direct the evolution of the universe?
- As we venture further into space, or listen better to what's out there, will we encounter other beings with designs of their own?[72]
- Will physics be reduced to mathematics? For example, are the laws of physics manifestations of mathematical symmetries?
- How will the elimination of disease and death affect selfhood and civilization?
- Is it true that "the poor will always be with us"? If we do succeed in eliminating *material* poverty, will there be new forms of scarcity—such as unequal sharing of information and knowledge—that divide rich and poor?
- What question do I have for each of my friends?
- Why is life hard?

The source of the memories in this memoir are the questions that impelled my quests. In conclusion, two questions for you:

What are your questions? What quests could lead to answers?

Epilogue | Who Wrote This? Who Is It About?

Je suis un autre.[73] – Arthur Rimbaud

The stark truth is that the person to whom the stories in this memoir refer no longer exists. That kid who wouldn't eat his spinach is gone—"dead" not to mince words—even though his passing was unremarked.

A writer may bear the same name as the subject of his memoir, but he is hardly the same person. He has long since morphed into the subject's successor, and then the successor of the successor.

Most memoirists are aware of this, but cheerfully proceed as if the teller of the tale and its protagonist were one and the same. Authors and readers alike collude in the reification of self, and then go on to assume that, like the Barbie doll or baseball glove in their closet, their self has persisted—as itself—for life. To admit to the non-existence of the beings we were, and remember fondly, is so unbearably sad that we delude ourselves with the unexamined assumption that selfhood is continuous and immutable. We even keep the self alive after death by positing an immortal soul.

I, the Bob Fuller who published this memoir, am not even the person who excavated these memories. The present me is more like the people I hang out with today than the fellow you've read about in this book.

There's an error of identification at the heart of the autobiographical and memoirist genres: the idea that, despite changes in appearance, experience, circumstances, and our synapses, the self we are today is that of the child in our family album who bears our name.

As we put memories into words, the words enshroud the memories. Before long, we are revisiting not the virgin memory, but our rendition of it. Thus do legends grow and memoirists slip the noose.

Acknowledgements

Mentors, Teachers, Allies, and Co-Creators

Mentors not only know more than we do, they know they know more, but they make nothing of it. We accept this asymmetry because we sense we're absorbing something priceless. As the etymology of the word suggests,[74] mentors take us to places we'd not get to without them.

Teachers convey the facts and show us how to organize them. They impart techniques and methods that equip us to undertake our own quests.

An ally is a colleague who supports, encourages, or partners with us to help us complete a task or get the best from ourselves.

Co-creators are anyone and everyone.

Mentors

- Calvin Souther Fuller,[75] humble fact-finder
- Willmine Works Fuller, formidable crusader
- Mr. Oliver Van Cise, teacher of democracy and coach
- Mr. Richard Lynch, Latin teacher at Chatham High School
- David Thomas, political theorist-activist and connoisseur
- Peter Funkhouser, kindhearted wordsmith
- Mary Alice Hughes and Ruth Garrett, tutors in Eros
- Judd Fermi, wise skeptic
- Peter Putnam,[76] model builder
- Laura Fermi,[77] grace personified
- John A. Wheeler,[78] natural philosopher
- I. Rabi,[79] impish sage
- Charles Huey, a man of few words and much authority
- Theodore D. Lockwood,[80] Taoist leader
- F. Champion Ward, Oberlin trustee, who took a chance on me
- John Reid, Oberlin trustee, steady helmsman in a storm
- Albert Bowker,[81] educational statesman
- Jean Klein, non-dual metaphysician

- Gordon Sherman,[82] Renaissance man
- Robert M. Cabot,[83] prince

Teachers

- Julius Quincy Fuller, grandfather, numerophile
- Marie Chilton Works, grandmother, peacemaker
- Miss Swenson, Mrs. Gail, Miss Belcher, Mrs. Bahoosian, Miss Stetler, Miss Catherine Burke, Miss Marie Burke, Mr. Vincent Finelli: my elementary school teachers from Kindergarten through seventh grade at Chatham Township Public School.
- Mrs. Smith, piano teacher and Mr. Aldrich, conductor of high school orchestra
- Jack Champlin, high school English teacher who put *Les Misérables* in my hands and told me to read it. Its protagonist, Jean Valjean, was a nobody who became a somebody who became a nobody who became immortal.
- Eldridge P. "Fuzzy" Vance and John Baum, exemplary math teachers at Oberlin College
- Jack Kneller, college French teacher, president of Brooklyn College
- Robert Ornstein, college English teacher
- Thurston Manning, college physics teacher
- Eduardo Mondlane, Founding Father of Mozambique
- Paul Halmos, author of math texts who promised to give away the secrets and did
- Dave Larson, problem-solver
- Collective apprenticeship with Fellows at Wesleyan's Center for Advanced Study: Stephen Spender,[84] poet; Paul Horgan,[85] writer; Richard Goodwin,[86] advisor to Presidents Kennedy and Johnson; I. A. Richards,[87] literary critic; William Arrowsmith,[88] classicist

- John Little, Seattle's own Bill Cosby
- Ruth Gruber, dance teacher
- Robert Kurtz, running coach
- Tommie Smith, gentle "militant," performance artist, and sprinting coach
- Toby Wells, Jack of all trades
- Mel Randall, philosopher of work

Allies

- Tom Purvis, fellow dreamer (from kindergarten on)
- Bill Dickinson and David Ford, playmates and teammates
- Pete Radcliffe and Tony Newcomb, fellow adventurers
- Ann Fuller, feminist pioneer and partner
- Daniel Greenberg, philosopher of education, founder of Sudbury Valley School
- Frederick W. Byron, Jr. and Pamela Gerloff, co-authors
- Delia Carol Pitts, personification of dignity and grace
- Karen Buck, peerless co-worker
- David Love, who found a question that shatters the myth of selfhood: *To what extent is a man obliged to keep promises made by a former self?*
- Güneli Gün, truth teller
- Zara Wallace, feminist seeker
- Alia Johnson, intrepid partner in exploration
- David Hoffman, fellow enthusiast
- Kim Spencer, media pioneer
- Evelyn Messinger, media visionary
- Tony Husch, asker of fertile questions
- John Hobbs, writing coach
- David Landau, brave intellectual
- Thomas J. Scheff, easy rider[89]

- Ina Cooper, impeccable editor
- Melanie Hart, designer of first breakingranks.net web site
- Elisa Cooper, Geek Friday
- Chuck Blitz, quester
- John Steiner, champion
- Claire Sheridan, editor nonpareil, companion, wife till death do us part

These acknowledgements are incomplete without making reference to the host of unnamed **co-creators**—living and dead, known and unknown—without whom no being, no becoming, no belonging.

Endnotes

[1] Arlene (family name unknown), Thomas Alexander Purvis, Jean Angle, David Robinson Mears, Bruce Hansen, William B. Dickinson, Linda Kennedy, John A. Bullock, Lucia H. Taylor (Holland), Eleanor Alma Weihermiller, Joan R. M. Weimer, Ronald Van Brunt, Gordon Long, Rudolf D. Kramm, Maude E. Stephens, Arthur Bontempo, Lawrence Wassil, Gertrude L. Morton, Sonya E. Peterson, Jerry Robertson, Robert Gerald Waterfield, Frederika E. Meiele, Jaap (Jack) Severeins (from Holland via Java in WW II), John England, Laura Lea Zander, Joeanna Ellicks (Clark), Gerald Harrsch, Sandra Cambon, Christine Stefani (Monett), Hank Osborne, Thomas Torgeson 3rd, Richard J. and William Scheuerman (twins), Robert Doll, Robert Marquardt, George G. Waterman, Jack Chester, Marilyn Speck, Eric (family name unknown).

[2] Gerald Pearson and Daryl Chapin.

[3] Building models, or Model-building—"modeling" for short—is described, and many examples are given, in *All Rise* and *Religion and Science*.

[4] A best-seller at the time was "30 Days to a More Powerful Vocabulary," by Wilfred Funk and Norman Lewis.

[5] With a nod to SpongeBob SquarePants, Nickelodeon's cartoon character.

[6] The issue remains unsettled, but seems close to resolution. See *What Is Life? How Chemistry Becomes Biology*, by Addy Pross (Oxford, 2012).

[7] Benedict de Spinoza, the Dutch philosopher of Jewish origin, (1632–77).

[8] Phil Anderson, John Bardeen, Walter Brattain, Richard Hamming, Conyers Herring, Walter Kohn, William Shockley, and my father's solar cell colleagues, Gerald Pearson, and Daryl Chapin.

[9] Charles Misner, who would go on to become one of the leading figures in general relativity. That summer, he introduced me to his classmate at Princeton, Hugh Everett III, who had just devised his theory of multiple universes and was eager to explain it to anyone who would listen. Everett, Misner, and I all worked with John A. Wheeler, who took the lead in reviving the study of general relativity and gravity after Einstein's death in 1955.

[10] Jon Gertner describes Bell Labs in its heyday in *The Idea Factory: Bell Labs and the Great Age of American Innovation* (Penguin Press, 2012).

[11] J. Mills Whitham, *A Biographical History of the French Revolution* (London: George Routledge& Sons, 1930).

[12] Stephen Potter, *One-Upmanship* (Kingston, RI: Asphodel Press, reprinted in 1997).

[13] Paul R. Halmos, *Finite Dimensional Vector Spaces* (New York: Springer Publishing Co., 1993).

[14] Arlene may have moved from Chatham to Hoboken, NJ, but there the trail goes cold.

[15] Henry Adams, *The Education of Henry Adams*, Chapter 21.

[16] ENS is the pinnacle of the French institutions of higher education. In some ways, it's the French counterpart of the elite colleges of Oxford and Cambridge in Britain. Some of its famous students (women were not admitted until late in the 20th century) include Louis Pasteur, Victor Cousin, Jean Jaurès, Evariste Galois, Jean Giraudoux, Léon Blum, Henri Bergson, Romain Rolland, Marc Block, Louis Althusser, Régis Dubray, Michel Foucault, Jules Lemaître, Émile Durkheim, Jacques Derrida, Georges Perec, Raymond Aron, Jean-Paul Sartre, Bernard-Henri Lévy, and eight French winners of the Fields Medal for mathematics. My impressions of it as a 21 year-old *pensionnaire étranger* were published in the Institute of International Education News Builletin, Vol. 33, No. 6 (February 1958).

[17] By Wolfgang K. H. Panofsky and Melba Phillips.

[18] Another professor associated with the Committee was Allan Bloom, author of the 1992 bestseller *The Closing of the American Mind*, and fictionalized by Saul Bellow as Ravelstein in his novel of that title.

[19] Peter A. Putnam (1926–1987) published only a few papers, although his private writings were voluminous. Some of them are housed in the library of Union Theological Seminary in New York City. Further information on Putnam can be found on a website devoted to his work: www.peterputnam.org. In 1967, Wesleyan University Press published something I wrote based on his work titled *Causal and Moral Law—Their Relationship as Examined in Terms of a Model of the Brain*, which appeared as Number 13 in a series of Monday Evening Papers presented at Wesleyan University's Center for Advanced Study. A related paper, co-authored with Peter Putnam, which outlines Putnam's Darwinian model of brain function, is titled *On the Origin of Order in Behavior*, and can be found in *General Systems*, Vol. XI, pp. 99–112 (1966), Mental Health Research

Institute, University of Michigan, Ann Arbor, Michigan. Attempts to bring Putnam's pioneering discoveries to the attention of other neuroscientists have been met with silence. He came from a well-to-do Cleveland family and had acquired a knack for making money in the stock market. Despite his family wealth, which he expanded considerably, he lived modestly, eating meager home-cooked meals of boiled potatoes and onions. When he died (in 1987), he left millions to educational and environmental institutions, and numerous unpublished manuscripts.

[20] Written by Russ Morgan, Larry Stock, and James Cavanaugh and published in 1944. Made famous by Dean Martin.

[21] Subsequently Harvard Junior Fellow and Professor of Chemistry at the University of California at Berkeley.

[22] Bohr and Wheeler predicted that Uranium 235, not the much more plentiful U 238, was the isotope with military significance. Wheeler's role in the Manhattan project was to oversee the industrial-level separation of these isotopes and so overcome this practical obstacle to developing nuclear weapons.

[23] *Causality and Multiply Connected Space-Time*, Physical Review, Vol 128, No. 2, pp. 919–929, October 15, 1962 by Robert W. Fuller and John A. Wheeler. Cited in Scientific American (January 2000, p.49) and in *The Fabric of the Cosmos* by Brian Greene (p. 467). The analysis applies only to objects with positive energy; time travel for objects of negative energy is not ruled out.

[24] John A. Wheeler died on April 13, 2008. About a year before his death, I sent him a message (dated June 26, 2007) c/o Ken Ford, another of John's students, who was then assisting him with correspondence. It read:

"Please tell John, that I think of him every day, as I imagine all his students do. I'd like to tell him how much his example has influenced my life and work over the years and how I hope I've put something of what I learned from him into the world.

"John's influence is apparent in my recent books—*Somebodies and Nobodies* and *All Rise*. They're not physics, but they do bear the stamp of "John Archibald Wheeler." His spirit pervades them.

"John might be interested to know that my core message—dignity for all—is one I caught a glimpse of while working with him at Princeton and Berkeley. Along with his contributions to physics, the impeccable example he set—of equal regard, dignity, and generosity—will outlive him."

²⁵ Noting the obituary for the inventor of Fortran (John W. Backus) in the *New York Times* (2007), I thought, *Without you, I'd have had a wholly different life.*

²⁶ Ernest Becker, *The Denial of Death* (Free Press, 1997).

²⁷ Reading Sabine's *Political Thought* while at Columbia was an echo of reading Carl Brent Swisher's *The Theory and Practice of American National Government* and Bishop & Hendel's *Basic Issues of American Democracy* during the summer between my freshman and sophomore years of college—an attempt to learn some civics, which I'd missed by leaving high school early.

²⁸ Daniel Greenberg describes the school he founded in: *Free at Last: The Sudbury Valley School.* It was inspired by A. S. Neill's school—Summerhill—founded in Britain in 1921, and described in Neill's book of that title.

²⁹ In addition to a talk in John Wheeler's living room to a group of Princeton graduate students and faculty, I presented Putnam's model at Columbia and Harvard Universities, The University of Texas (Austin), Ohio State, Penn State, The University of California (Irvine), and The State University of New York (Stony Brook), The University of Massachusetts (Amherst), Wesleyan University, and Battelle Memorial Institute in Columbus, OH. Putnam presented his model at the Union Theological Seminary in New York City.

³⁰ *On the Origin of Order in Behavior, General Systems*, Vol. XI, pp. 99–112 (1966), Mental Health Research Institute, University of Michigan, Ann Arbor, Michigan.

³¹ http://www.peterputnam.org is a website devoted to Peter Putnam's life and work. It was created by Barry Spinello, one of the students Putnam mentored.

³² Paul Horgan, *Great River: The Rio Grande in North American History* (Wesleyan, 1991).

³³ Paul Gallico's first work of fiction after leaving sports—*The Snow Goose*—is regarded by some as a masterpiece. And, I am happy that *Mathematics of Classical and Quantum Physics* is still in print more than fifty years after I first taught the course at Columbia in 1961.

³⁴ Until recently it was believed that their relative invulnerability to skin cancer gave dark-skinned people a reproductive advantage; but

recent research indicates it is rather that darker skin prevents ultraviolet radiation from destroying a key nutrient of reproductive success—the B vitamin folate.

[35] Novelists do this. Think, for example, of the interior monologues of James Joyce's and Virginia Woolf's characters. Overhearing Mrs. Dalloway's thoughts strengthened the witness in me.

[36] I've benefitted from many editors—for example, John Steiner, Tony Husch, Thomas Purvis, Peter Sharp, David Landau, Edwin Taylor, Janet Coleman, Johanna Vondeling, and Robert Cabot. Three editors, who've served me as longstanding, formative mentors, are John Hobbs, Ina Cooper, and Claire Sheridan.

[37] Cass Jackson, Tommie Smith, and Patrick Penn, respectively. Cosell's broadcast is available on YouTube: http://www.youtube.com/watch?v=LPZerZXTNX0

[38] Likely an ancestor of mine; in any case, someone with whom I see eye-to-eye on the pluses and minuses of travel.

[39] Richard Feynman was John Wheeler's first and most famous graduate student. He developed a suggestion of Wheeler's into a reframing of quantum theory, which he successfully applied to outstanding problems in quantum electrodynamics for which he was awarded a Nobel Prize. Towards the end of his life, Feynman came to public attention as the quirky scientist on the panel investigating the Challenger shuttle disaster who explained the explosion on national television as due to frozen O-rings.

[40] For example, Jean Klein, Nisargadatta, Wei Wu Wei, Douglas Harding, Hubert Benoit (and the commentary on his work by John H. G. Pierson), John Levy, Erwin Schrödinger, Walter Truett Anderson, Chögyam Trungpa, Ram Dass, Franklin Merritt-Wolff, Atmananda, Joel Kramer, Robert Powell, Alan Watts, Ramana Maharshi, et al.

[41] The film, *The Hungry Planet*, was made by Keith Blume of the Planet Earth Foundation (Seattle), with assistance from Roy Prosterman of the University of Washington and the participation of singer-songwriter Harry Chapin.

[42] *To the Finland Station*, Edmund Wilson (Lightyear, 2000).

[43] David Hoffman, Kim Spencer, and John Steiner.

[44] David Hunter's obituary in the *New York Times*: http://query.nytimes.com/gst/fullpage.html?res=9E00E7D7123D F933A05752C1A9669C8B63

[45] An interview with this title was published by the *Christian Science Monitor* (Dec. 16, 1982, p. B6) and also by *Evolutionary Blues*, Vol. 2, 1983, and reprinted widely in several languages. The gist of the interview is implicit in its title.

[46] Motzu's philosophy is presented in *Mo Tzu: Basic Writings* as translated by Burton Watson, Columbia University Press (New York, 1963). In China, Mo Tzu is written Mo Zi.

[47] We lived at 2248 Summer St. (which we later discovered had been the boyhood home of Robert Culp, who, with Bill Cosby, helped break down racial barriers in television in the drama *I Spy*). In 1988, we sold the house to Les Blank, the documentary filmmaker, who died in 2013.

[48] Robert Cabot's groundbreaking novel is titled *The Joshua Tree* (Atheneum 1970). Our joint articles, published in *The Harvard Review*, are *The Asian Vortex* (November 1987) and *Empire's End, Russia's Rebirth* (May-June 1991). A prediction in the latter paper—the dissolution of the Soviet Union and its satellite empire—had in fact been anticipated by a prescient and insightful political forecast: *Decline of an Empire: The Soviet Socialist Republics in Revolt* by Hélène Carrère d'Encausse (1981).

[49] In addition to Alia Johnson and me (and our two kids, Noah and Adam, who accompanied us on most of the trips), there were Kim Spencer and Evelyn Messinger, David Hoffman and Sharon Nelson, Marlow Hotchkiss and Cynthia Jurs, John Steiner and Margo King, Sara Leslie Conover, and Fran "Finley" Peavey (who stationed herself on park benches around the world with a banner that read: **American Willing to Listen**).

[50] The Donuts evolved into a non-profit called The Threshold Foundation.

[51] "Never to Forget" is the title of a book of poems by my great uncle, Eugene White Fuller (Ralph Fletcher Seymour, Publisher, Chicago, IL, 1948).

[52] *Their titles were A Better Game than War; Question/Answer Book; The Future of Equality; Travels in Nobodyland: Questing for Identity; and an allegory for children called Theo, the White Squirrel.*

[53] These ideas later figured centrally in three books: *Somebodies and Nobodies: Overcoming the Abuse of Rank* (New Society Publishers, British Columbia, 2003); *All Rise: Somebodies, Nobodies, and the Politics of Dignity* (Berrett-Koehler Publishers, San Francisco, 2006); and, co-authored with

Pamela A. Gerloff, *Dignity for All: How to Create a World without Rankism* (Berrett-Koehler Publishers, San Francisco, 2008).

[54] Ridhwan School.

[55] Prostate specific antigen.

[56] Claire Sheridan founded the innovative LEAP program to empower professional dancers by providing them with a college education tailored to the demands of their careers as performers. For more on LEAP: http://www.stmarys-ca.edu/leap

[57] Upon the advice of several female athletes, it has been decided that women should be allotted an extra 20 seconds at any age. As I grow older, I'm thinking that men should be allotted and extra 10 or 20 seconds, too. Whatever the criterion, it should be chosen so that getting into the club requires an aspirant to optimize a number of fitness factors: speed and stamina, of course, but also upper-body strength, weight, and flexibility.

[58] Despite numerous recommendations, from somebodies and nobodies alike, to Oprah's producers, the phone has not rung. In her long-running TV show, Oprah took up every ism but one—rankism— the mother of them all.

[59] *Doing Democracy* (Gabriola Island, B.C.: New Society Publishers, 2001) by Bill Moyer, is a widely-used practical handbook on movement politics.

[60] The Beijing World Publishing Corporation is publishing *Somebodies and Nobodies* in Chinese translation in 2014.

[61] Terkel had come to Oberlin while I was president in the early seventies to tape a TV show he hosted called "The Great American Dream Machine."

[62] Studs Terkel's endorsement follows in full. The italicized words were used by the publisher on the cover of *Somebodies and Nobodies*.

"I've been disturbed, especially during the past several years, by my restaurant encounters. The servers invariably wear an ID: Barbara or James. I, as patron, am always addressed with the prefix "Mr." I've always made a point to ask "What's your last name?" I'm not out to make trouble, just curious. The server often mumbles, as though embarrassed, his or her surname.

Consider this a metaphor for the theme of Robert Fuller's *wonderful and tremendously important book on the 'ism' that is far more encompassing than racism, sexism or ageism. Rankism must be our prime target from now on in. Viva Fuller!"*

63 This point of view is elaborated in *The Moral Arc of History*, published in a Festschrift for Michael Murphy titled *An Actual Man*, and also in the journal Cadmus (Fall, 2011).

64 The concept of "menome" is explained in *Genomes, Menomes, Wenomes: Neuroscience and Human Dignity*, available for free at :https://www.smashwords.com/books/view/332823

65 The Viveka Foundation published an Indian edition of *All Rise* in 2007.

66 *All Rise* was published in Bangla in 2009. In 2011, at the invitation of the President of Bangladesh, I delivered the keynote address at a "Dignity for All" conference he hosted.

67 The Shanghai Peoples Publishing House published *All Rise* in Chinese translation in 2008.

68 *The Moral Arc of the Universe*. http://www.huffingtonpost.com/robert-fuller/the-moral-arc-of-the-universe_b_3239412.html. As cited above, this essay is also available in the scholarly journal, CADMUS, Vol.1, Issue 3 (October 2011): http://cadmusjournal.org/content/volume1-issue3-october-2011.

69 *Religion and Science: A Beautiful Friendship?* Free download at Amazon Kindle and at https://www.smashwords.com/books/view/209786 This book was also broken up into twenty blog posts and serialized in 2012 at: thehuffingtonpost.com, psychologytoday.com, dailykos.com, firedoglake.com, newsvine.com, themoderatevoice.com, beliefnet.com, christianblog.com, talk2action.com, opensalon.com, laprogressive.com, and breakingranks.net. I've also published an ebook titled *Genomes, Menomes, Wenomes: Neuroscience and Human Dignity* that aims to buttress the case for treating dignity as a universal right by showing that selfhood is inherently communal, that being is inseparable from belonging, and that all creations are co-creations.

70 *The Imitation of our Lord Don Quixote*, Simon Leys, *The New York Review of Books*, Vol. XLV, No. 10, pp. 32–35 (June 11, 1998). Leys acknowledges paraphrasing George Bernard Shaw, so here I'm paraphrasing a paraphrase.

71 Danny Hillis, a computer scientist famously said, "I want to build a machine who is proud of me."

72 According to legend, when asked what his first question would be if he returned to life in 500 years, Einstein volunteered, "Is the Universe friendly?"

73 I am an other.

74 After Mentor, advisor of Odysseus and tutor of Telemachus in Homer's *Odyssey*, from the Latin.

75 John Perlin gives an account of C.S. Fuller's co-invention (with Gerald Pearson and Daryl Chapin) of the solar cell in *From Space to Earth: The Story of Solar Energy* (Harvard University Press, 2002).

76 Website: www.peterputnam.org.

77 Laura Fermi, *Atoms in the Family* (Universiy of Chicago Press, 1985).

78 *Geons, Black Holes & Quantum Foam: A Life in Physics*, John A. Wheeler with Kenneth Ford (Norton, 1998).

79 *Rabi: Scientist and Citizen*, John S. Rigden (Harvard University Press, 2000).

80 President of Trinity College, Hartford, CN, 1968–1981.

81 Albert Bowker, See http://www.stat.berkeley.edu/~bowker/

82 Gordon Sherman, President of Midas Muffler during its expansion via franchising.

83 Robert Cabot, soldier, sailor, diplomat, philanthropist, novelist (*The Joshua Tree, That Sweetest Wine, The Isle of Khería*). My book *Somebodies and Nobodies* owes its existence to Cabot, and so is dedicated to him.

84 Stephen Spender, *World Within World* (Modern Library, 2001).

85 Paul Horgan, Pulitzer prize-winning author of *Great River: The Rio Grande in North American History*.

86 Richard N. Goodwin, advisor and speechwriter to Presidents Kennedy and Johnson and to Senator Robert F. Kennedy.

87 I. A. Richards, co-creator of Basic English.

88 For a vignette of Arrowsmith by Saul Bellow see: *It All Adds Up* (Penguin Books, 1995), pp. 280–283.

89 Thomas Scheff, long-time chairman of Sociology Department at UC-Santa Barbara. His memoir is titled: Easy Rider: Poems, Essays, and Memoir (iUniverse, Inc. 2007).

About the Author

Robert W. Fuller earned his Ph.D. in physics at Princeton University and taught at Columbia, where he co-authored *Mathematics of Classical and Quantum Physics*. He then served as president of Oberlin College, his alma mater. For a dozen years, beginning in 1978, he worked in what came to be known as "citizen diplomacy" to improve the Cold War relationship. During the 1990s, he served as board chair of the global NGO Internews, which promotes democracy via free and independent media. In 2004 he was elected a Fellow of the World Academy of Art and Science, and in 2011 he served as keynote speaker at the National Conference on Dignity for All hosted by the president of Bangladesh. With the end of the Cold War and the collapse of the USSR, Fuller looked back on his career and understood that he had been, at different times in his life, a somebody and a nobody. His periodic sojourns into "Nobodyland" led him to identify and probe rankism—abuse of the power inherent in rank—and ultimately to write *Somebodies and Nobodies: Overcoming the Abuse of Rank* (New Society Publishers, 2003). Three years later, he published a sequel focusing on building a "dignitarian" society, titled *All Rise: Somebodies, Nobodies, and the Politics of Dignity* (Berrett-Koehler, 2006). An Indian edition was published in 2007 (Viveka Foundation), a Chinese translation in 2008, and a Bengali translation in 2009. With co-author Pamela Gerloff, Fuller has also published *Dignity for All: How to Create a World Without Rankism*. His most recent books are *Religion and Science: A Beautiful Friendship?*, *From Genome to Wenome: The Key to Universal Dignity*, and *The Rowan Tree: A Novel*.

Connect with Robert W. Fuller Online

Web site: www.robertworksfuller.com
Facebook: www.facebook.com/robertwfuller
Twitter: twitter.com/#!/robertwfuller

For readers who want to explore dignity as a foundation for interpersonal and international relations, Robert W. Fuller's novel The Rowan Tree is now available as an ebook, a paperback, and an audiobook at: www.rowantreenovel.com

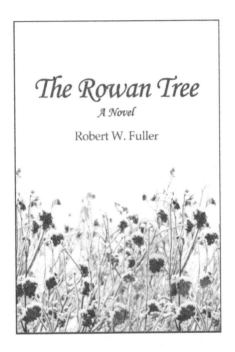

As Arthurian myth sowed seeds of democracy, The Rowan Tree foretells an international culture of dignity. Anchored by two interlocking love stories, this unflinching novel of ideas brims with passionate quests, revelatory failures, and inextinguishable hope.

The Rowan Tree is an inspirational tour de force that reaches from the rebellious American '60s into humanity's global future. Soul-searching treks around the world intersect with campus revolution, basketball, math, ballet, and a destined rise to the White House. Love runs ahead of politics and lights the way for nations to follow.

Made in the USA
Middletown, DE
29 December 2020